SCIENTIFIC AMERICAN EXPLORES BIG IDEAS

Science's Greatest Mysteries

The Editors of *Scientific American*

SCIENTIFIC AMERICAN | EDUCATIONAL PUBLISHING

New York

Published in 2025 by Scientific American Educational Publishing
in association with The Rosen Publishing Group
2544 Clinton Street, Buffalo NY 14224

Contains material from Scientific American®, a division of Springer Nature America, Inc., reprinted by permission, as well as original material from The Rosen Publishing Group®.

Copyright © 2025 Scientific American® and Rosen Publishing Group®.

All rights reserved.

First Edition

Scientific American
Lisa Pallatroni: Project Editor

Rosen Publishing
Michael Hessel-Mial: Compiling Editor
Michael Moy: Senior Graphic Designer

Cataloging-in-Publication Data

Names: Scientific American, Inc.
Title: Science's greatest mysteries / edited by the Scientific American Editors.
Description: First edition. | New York : Scientific American Educational Publishing, 2025. | Series: Scientific American explores big ideas | Includes bibliographic references and index.
Identifiers: ISBN 9781538312926 (pbk.) | ISBN 9781538312933 (library bound)| ISBN 9781538312940 (ebook)
Subjects: LCSH: Science–Miscellanea–Juvenile literature. | Discoveries in science–Miscellanea–Juvenile literature.
Classification: LCC Q163.S354 2025 | DDC 500–dc23

Manufactured in the United States of America
Websites listed were live at the time of publication.

Cover: Gorodenkoff/Shutterstock.com

CPSIA Compliance Information: Batch # CW25SA.
For Further Information contact Rosen Publishing at 1-800-237-9932.

CONTENTS

Introduction 5

Section 1: Life and Evolution 6

1.1 The First Gene on Earth May Have Been a Hybrid 7
By Andy Extance

1.2 The Future of Man—How Will Evolution Change Humans? 12
By Peter Ward

1.3 Evidence Implies That Animals Feel Empathy 22
By Frans B. M. de Waal

1.4 The Search for Extraterrestrial Life as We Don't Know It 30
By Sarah Scoles

Section 2: Physics Mysteries 44

2.1 The Weirdest Particles in the Universe 45
By Clara Moskowitz

2.2 Why Aren't We Made of Antimatter? 50
By Luke Caldwell

2.3 Something Is Wrong with Dark Energy, Physicists Say 61
By Rebecca Boyle

Section 3: Health and the Mind 69

3.1 Schizophrenia's Unyielding Mysteries 70
By Michael Balter

3.2 What's So Funny? The Science of Why We Laugh 83
By Giovanni Sabato

3.3 How Old Can Humans Get? 92
By Bill Gifford

Section 4: Human Nature 97

4.1 What's the World's Oldest Language? 98
By Lucy Tu

4.2	War Is *Not* Part of Human Nature By R. Brian Ferguson	102
4.3	Is Inequality Inevitable? By Bruce M. Boghosian	112
4.4	The Theory That Men Evolved to Hunt and Women Evolved to Gather Is Wrong By Cara Ocobock & Sarah Lacy	122

Section 5: Earth's Strangest Places — 132

5.1	Volcanic Activity, Not Giant Bears, Created Enigmatic Devils Tower By Scott K. Johnson	133
5.2	Ocean Discoveries Are Revising Long-Held Truths about Life By Timothy Shank	136
5.3	'Dark Oxygen' Discovered Coming from Mineral Deposits on Deep Seafloor By Allison Parshall	139
5.4	One Mystery of Stonehenge's Origins Has Finally Been Solved By Scott Hershberger	144
5.5	King Tut Mysteries Endure 100 Years after Discovery By Zach Zorich	147

Glossary — 153
Further Information — 155
Citations — 156
Index — 157

INTRODUCTION

There's something powerful in recognizing a phenomenon that resists easy explanation. Such phenomena get our minds to work, inspiring conversations where friends can speculate or argue about possible answers. The weirdness of the universe makes all of us equals in trying to understand. For many scientists, these mysteries inspired them to take up the labor of research in the first place. The articles in this title cover some of these fascinating, perplexing questions. Where does life come from? Does alien life exist? What is the universe made of, and why? Why do we laugh? Why do we die? Why do people treat one another so badly sometimes?

These scientific mysteries are organized into five major sections. The first section explores questions related to biology. The second focuses on current dilemmas in physics and astronomy. The third section is about health and the human body. The fourth covers questions of human nature: language, inequality, and conflict. The fifth tours some of Earth's strange phenomena.

As you read, you'll find that something interesting happens. The big, broad, exciting questions change into more focused, specific research questions. These questions become the basis of experiments, taking the work of finding an answer away from private conversation into a larger public labor of understanding. This practice is largely how scientists have always responded to these challenging questions, and shows how discoveries always begin with a mystery.

Of the questions this book explores, many remain unanswered. However, some are, with the mystery translated by research into scientific laws we can understand. There might be a sense of loss, but with it comes the gain of knowledge that can help discover new cures, inventions, and possibly new forms of life.

Section 1: Life and Evolution

1.1 The First Gene on Earth May Have Been a Hybrid
By Andy Extance

1.2 The Future of Man—How Will Evolution Change Humans?
By Peter Ward

1.3 Evidence Implies That Animals Feel Empathy
By Frans B. M. de Waal

1.4 The Search for Extraterrestrial Life as We Don't Know It
By Sarah Scoles

The First Gene on Earth May Have Been a Hybrid

By Andy Extance

DNA and RNA, the two major modern forms of genetic code underpinning all of earthly biology, could have coexisted in strict pairings on our planet before life arose here, scientists in England, Scotland and Poland say. Using a hydrogen cyanide–based chemical system intended to mimic conditions in Earth's early history, the researchers made four bases, the molecular "letters" of the genetic alphabet. Strung together, these bases form gene sequences that cells translate into proteins. But surprisingly, the team found that of the four bases their experiments consistently made, two were in a form found in DNA, whereas the other two were of a kind seen in RNA.

The study, published in *Nature* and conducted by John Sutherland of the Medical Research Council Laboratory of Molecular Biology in Cambridge, England, and his colleagues, further undermines the so-called RNA world hypothesis. This idea, long one of the most prominent in origins-of-life research, posits that RNA formed the basis of Earth's biosphere long before DNA and other molecules important to life emerged. Yet to date, scant evidence has been found of chemical pathways to make the RNA-exclusive system that rigid versions of the idea adopt or that could lead to DNA. "People have tended to think of RNA as the parent of DNA," Sutherland says. "This [paper] suggests that they are molecular siblings."

Other scientists who were not involved with the study question the plausibility of the conditions used in this hydrogen cyanide-based route, however. Frances Westall, director of the exobiology group at the French National Center for Scientific Research's Center for Molecular Biophysics in Orléans, notes that forming the bases requires very specific conditions. Mixtures would need to dry out and be exposed to ultraviolet light—two hurdles most easily surmounted on dry land, which was in short supply during our planet's ocean-covered early days more than four billion years ago. "These conditions certainly existed on the early Earth," Westall says. "They would not have been that common because there was not that much exposed landmass." Although she adds that the study is "clever" and "not completely impossible," she concludes that "there are other, better hypotheses as to locations for the emergence of life and prebiotic molecules."

Arguments about plausibility have plagued the chemistry-based quest to understand life's beginnings on Earth since the early 1950s, when American researchers Stanley Miller and Harold Urey performed a landmark experiment. The pair simulated the effects of lightning in the early Earth's atmosphere and ocean by triggering electrical discharges in flasks containing hydrogen, water, ammonia and methane. Although their experiment famously produced sizable organic molecules vital for biochemistry, for decades other researchers have debated the plausibility of its conditions. Nevertheless, Miller and Urey's work showed that it was relatively simple to make important substances, such as the amino acids that link up to form proteins that perform myriad functions within living cells. Of particular relevance to origins-of-life studies, proteins can act as catalysts, enhancing and speeding up other chemical reactions that would otherwise be too slow or inefficient to plausibly occur. But proteins are not the only possible catalysts behind the rise of life on Earth.

In work that would ultimately net the 1989 Nobel Prize in Chemistry, molecular biologist Sidney Altman and biochemist Thomas Cech found that RNA—long considered merely an intermediate carrier of genetic information that is subservient to DNA—can also behave as a catalyst. The RNA world hypothesis suggests that such molecules could self-replicate, enabling early evolution before the existence of DNA and proteins. The idea, however, "was an overzealous, overenthusiastic response to a brilliant discovery," Sutherland says.

That response might have come partly because, to a naive chemist, it looks easy to leap from RNA to DNA. To create the long chains we often see coiled up into the DNA's iconic double helix, the bases are first connected to a "backbone" of sugar molecules. These combinations make up nucleosides: deoxyribonucleotides in DNA and ribonucleosides in RNA—which, unlike its DNA cousin, forms a single helix. The nucleosides do not use table sugar, or sucrose, but rather ribose in RNA and deoxyribose in DNA (the different sugars give each material its first initial). The distinction between the two sugar types is tiny: just one oxygen and one hydrogen atom. Yet that difference is enough for DNA and RNA to have distinct biological roles. And biochemically removing the atoms is far harder than simply erasing the letters representing them in a notebook.

Another flaw in the RNA world idea has been the difficulty of making ribose in the conditions that probably existed on the early Earth—and to then connect it to a base. Sutherland and his colleagues therefore sought more likely ways to make ribose sugars and ribonucleosides. One of their most promising approaches relied on two gases thought to have been relatively abundant in the planet's early atmosphere: hydrogen sulfide and hydrogen cyanide. When dissolved in water, bathed in ultraviolet light and subjected to cycles of drying, these simple compounds have produced many more complex molecules. They include amino acids and glycerol, the backbones of fatty molecules that can form cells' outer wall.

Sutherland took this approach a step further last year. Working with Ramanarayanan Krishnamurthy's team at the Scripps Research Institute in La Jolla, Calif., he and his colleagues showed that the ribonucleosides cytidine and uridine could be transformed into deoxyribose and the nucleoside and deoxyadenosine. Now—primarily via the efforts of team members Jianfeng Xu and Václav Chmela, both then at the Laboratory of Molecular Biology—the researchers have made even more progress. They mixed some of the intermediate molecules from the team's previous studies with salts such as sodium nitrite and magnesium chloride that could have been prevalent on the primordial Earth, then subjected them to acidic conditions and heat, respectively. Through these steps, the scientists found two possible routes to add a fourth base, the less common nucleoside inosine, to their preexisting collection. The addition was enough to make a four-letter genetic alphabet in which each base in a strand would exclusively pair with one of the other three letters in a second strand. That base-pairing complementarity is how modern RNA and DNA works. But in the experiment, two letters came from RNA, and two came from DNA.

The arrangement "suggests that the chemistry to make RNA and DNA isn't as different as people have thought," Sutherland says. "People have tended to think of RNA coming before DNA and somehow then being taken over. This, to me, is suggesting that it's possible that you could have had an RNA-DNA hybrid, which could then give rise to the two separate molecules." Sutherland's team has not yet assembled the individual nucleosides and ribonucleosides into longer chains, however. Doing so is important, because showing that hybrid strands can really form and bind to a partner strand is crucial for moving the idea beyond speculation.

This is a key issue for Nicholas Hud, an origins-of-life researcher at the Georgia Institute of Technology, who was not involved in the study. He calls it an "excellent compilation of organic chemistry research" on water-based nucleoside synthesis. But Hud is not convinced that the paper resolves whether these nucleosides actually arose before living creatures. His own research suggests amino acids could have linked up to carry information and act as a catalyst before RNA. Hud thinks evolution would then have gradually produced the current genetic system over long stretches of geologic time. "If a molecule looks very difficult, from a chemical perspective, to make, yet it functions exquisitely in biology, then it's probably the case that it has been evolved over time," he says. For the same reasons, he is also skeptical about the RNA world hypothesis.

Furthermore, Hud sees the new study's reliance on rigid incremental steps, each performed in strict order and under carefully controlled conditions, as a significant weakness. If the order of the steps changed or certain products were not isolated, Sutherland and his colleagues would have made much less of the substances they are interested in, Hud says. That caveat reduces the chances of the scenario unfolding in the chaotic environs of the early Earth.

Section 1: Life and Evolution

Sutherland admits that, absent a time machine to travel back to life's true origins on our planet, "plausibility is everything" in this rarefied field of research. Even so, he firmly backs his team's work on establishing chemical routes to life's building blocks. "There are many, many fingers pointing at hydrogen cyanide," Sutherland asserts. "Does it prove that it all happened from hydrogen cyanide? It doesn't prove it. But it's good enough for me."

The Future of Man—How Will Evolution Change Humans?

By Peter Ward

When you ask for opinions about what future humans might look like, you typically get one of two answers. Some people trot out the old science-fiction vision of a big-brained human with a high forehead and higher intellect. Others say humans are no longer evolving physically—that technology has put an end to the brutal logic of natural selection and that evolution is now purely cultural.

The big-brain vision has no real scientific basis. The fossil record of skull sizes over the past several thousand generations shows that our days of rapid increase in brain size are long over. Accordingly, most scientists a few years ago would have taken the view that human physical evolution has ceased. But DNA techniques, which probe genomes both present and past, have unleashed a revolution in studying evolution; they tell a different story. Not only has *Homo sapiens* been doing some major genetic reshuffling since our species formed, but the rate of human evolution may, if anything, have increased. In common with other organisms, we underwent the most dramatic changes to our body shape when our species first appeared, but we continue to show genetically induced changes to our physiology and perhaps to our behavior as well. Until fairly recently in our history, human races in various parts of the world were becoming more rather than less distinct. Even today the conditions of modern life could be driving changes to genes for certain behavioral traits.

If giant brains are not in store for us, then what is? Will we become larger or smaller, smarter or dumber? How will the emergence of new diseases and the rise in global temperature shape us? Will a new human species arise one day? Or does the future evolution of humanity lie not within our genes but within our technology, as we augment our brains and bodies with silicon and steel? Are we but the builders of the next dominant intelligence on the earth—the machines?

The Far and Recent Past

Tracking human evolution used to be the province solely of paleontologists, those of us who study fossil bones from the ancient past. The human family, called the *Hominidae*, goes back at least seven million years to the appearance of a small proto-human called *Sahelanthropus tchadensis*.

Since then, our family has had a still disputed, but rather diverse, number of new species in it—as many as nine that we know of and others surely still hidden in the notoriously poor hominid fossil record. Because early human skeletons rarely made it into sedimentary rocks before they were scavenged, this estimate changes from year to year as new discoveries and new interpretations of past bones make their way into print.

Each new species evolved when a small group of hominids somehow became separated from the larger population for many generations and then found itself in novel environmental conditions favoring a different set of adaptations. Cut off from kin, the small population went its own genetic route and eventually its members could no longer successfully reproduce with the parent population.

The fossil record tells us that the oldest member of our own species lived 195,000 years ago in what is now Ethiopia. From there it spread out across the globe. By 10,000 years ago modern humans had successfully colonized each of the continents save Antarctica, and adaptations to these many locales (among other evolutionary forces) led to what we loosely call races. Groups living in different places evidently retained just enough connections with one another to avoid evolving into separate species. With the globe fairly well covered, one might expect that the time for evolving was pretty much finished.

But that turns out not to be the case. In a study published a year ago Henry C. Harpending of the University of Utah, John

Hawks of the University of Wisconsin–Madison and their colleagues analyzed data from the international haplotype map of the human genome. They focused on genetic markers in 270 people from four groups: Han Chinese, Japanese, Yoruba and northern Europeans. They found that at least 7 percent of human genes underwent evolution as recently as 5,000 years ago. Much of the change involved adaptations to particular environments, both natural and human-shaped. For example, few people in China and Africa can digest fresh milk into adulthood, whereas almost everyone in Sweden and Denmark can. This ability presumably arose as an adaptation to dairy farming.

Another study by Pardis C. Sabeti of Harvard University and her colleagues used huge data sets of genetic variation to look for signs of natural selection across the human genome. More than 300 regions on the genome showed evidence of recent changes that improved people's chance of surviving and reproducing. Examples included resistance to one of Africa's great scourges, the virus causing Lassa fever; partial resistance to other diseases, such as malaria, among some African populations; changes in skin pigmentation and development of hair follicles among Asians; and the evolution of lighter skin and blue eyes in northern Europe.

Harpending and Hawks's team estimated that over the past 10,000 years humans have evolved as much as 100 times faster than at any other time since the split of the earliest hominid from the ancestors of modern chimpanzees. The team attributed the quickening pace to the variety of environments humans moved into and the changes in living conditions brought about by agriculture and cities. It was not farming per se or the changes in the landscape that conversion of wild habitat to tamed fields brought about but the often lethal combination of poor sanitation, novel diet and emerging diseases (from other humans as well as domesticated animals). Although some researchers have expressed reservations about these estimates, the basic point seems clear: humans are first-class evolvers.

Unnatural Selection

During the past century, our species' circumstances have again changed. The geographic isolation of different groups has been broached by the ease of transportation and the dismantling of social barriers that once kept racial groups apart. Never before has the human gene pool had such widespread mixing of what were heretofore entirely separated local populations of our species. In fact, the mobility of humanity might be bringing about the homogenization of our species. At the same time, natural selection in our species is being thwarted by our technology and our medicines. In most parts of the globe, babies no longer die in large numbers. People with genetic damage that was once fatal now live and have children. Natural predators no longer affect the rules of survival.

Steve Jones of University College London has argued that human evolution has essentially ceased. At a Royal Society of Edinburgh debate in 2002 entitled "Is Evolution Over?" he said: "Things have simply stopped getting better, or worse, for our species. If you want to know what Utopia is like, just look around—this is it." Jones suggested that, at least in the developed world, almost everyone has the opportunity to reach reproductive age, and the poor and rich have an equal chance of having children. Inherited disease resistance—say, to HIV—may still confer a survival advantage, but culture, rather than genetic inheritance, is now the deciding factor in whether people live or die. In short, evolution may now be memetic—involving ideas—rather than genetic.

Another point of view is that genetic evolution continues to occur even today, but in reverse. Certain characteristics of modern life may drive evolutionary change that does not make us fitter for survival—or that even makes us less fit. Innumerable college students have noticed one potential way that such "inadaptive" evolution could happen: they put off reproduction while many of their high school classmates who did not make the grade started having babies right away. If less intelligent parents have more kids, then intelligence is a Darwinian liability in today's world, and average intelligence might evolve downward.

Such arguments have a long and contentious history. One of the many counterarguments is that human intelligence is made up of many different abilities encoded by a large number of genes. It thus has a low degree of heritability, the rate at which one generation passes the trait to the next. Natural selection acts only on heritable traits. Researchers actively debate just how heritable intelligence is, but they have found no sign that average intelligence is in fact decreasing.

Even if intelligence is not at risk, some scientists speculate that other, more heritable traits could be accumulating in the human species and that these traits are anything but good for us. For instance, behavior disorders such as Tourette's syndrome and attention-deficit hyperactivity disorder (ADHD) may, unlike intelligence, be encoded by but a few genes, in which case their heritability could be very high. If these disorders increase one's chance of having children, they could become ever more prevalent with each generation. David Comings, a specialist in these two diseases, has argued in scientific papers and a 1996 book that these conditions are more common than they used to be and that evolution might be one reason: women with these syndromes are less likely to attend college and thus tend to have more children than those who do not. But other researchers have brought forward serious concerns about Comings's methodology. It is not clear whether the incidence of Tourette's and ADHD is, in fact, increasing at all. Research into these areas is also made more difficult because of the perceived social stigma that many of these afflictions attach to their carriers.

Although these particular examples do not pass scientific muster, the basic line of reasoning is plausible. We tend to think of evolution as something involving structural modification, yet it can and does affect things invisible from the outside—behavior. Many people carry the genes making them susceptible to alcoholism, drug addiction and other problems. Most do not succumb, because genes are not destiny; their effect depends on our environment. But others do succumb, and their problems may affect whether they survive and how many children they have. These changes in fertility are enough for natural selection to act on. Much of humanity's future evolution may involve new sets of behaviors that spread in response to changing social and environmental conditions. Of course, humans differ from other species in that we do not have to accept this Darwinian logic passively.

Directed Evolution

We have directed the evolution of so many animal and plant species. Why not direct our own? Why wait for natural selection to do the job when we can do it faster and in ways beneficial to ourselves? In the area of human behavior, for example, geneticists are tracking down the genetic components not just of problems and disorders but also of overall disposition and various aspects of sexuality and competitiveness, many of which may be at least partially heritable. Over time, elaborate screening for genetic makeup may become commonplace, and people will be offered drugs based on the results.

The next step will be to actually change people's genes. That could conceivably be done in two ways: by changing genes in the relevant organ only (gene therapy) or by altering the entire genome of an individual (what is known as germ-line therapy). Researchers are still struggling with the limited goal of gene therapy to cure disease. But if they can ever pull off germ-line therapy, it will help not only the individual in question but also his or her children. The major obstacle to genetic engineering in humans will be the sheer complexity of the genome. Genes usually perform more than one function; conversely, functions are usually encoded by more than one gene. Because of this property, known as pleiotropy, tinkering with one gene can have unintended consequences.

Why try at all, then? The pressure to change genes will probably come from parents wanting to guarantee their child is a boy or a girl; to endow their children with beauty, intelligence, musical talent or a sweet nature; or to try to ensure that they are not helplessly disposed to become mean-spirited, depressed, hyperactive or even criminal. The motives are there, and they are very strong. Just as the push by parents to genetically enhance their children could be socially irresistible, so, too, would be an assault on human aging. Many recent studies suggest that aging is not so much a simple wearing down of body parts as it is a programmed decay, much of it genetically controlled. If so, the next century of genetic research could unlock numerous genes controlling many aspects of aging. Those genes could be manipulated.

Assuming that it does become practical to change our genes, how will that affect the future evolution of humanity? Probably a great deal. Suppose parents alter their unborn children to enhance their intelligence, looks and longevity. If the kids are as smart as they are long-lived—an IQ of 150 and a lifespan of 150 years—they could have more children and accumulate more wealth than the rest of us. Socially they will probably be drawn to others of their kind. With some kind of self-imposed geographic or social segregation, their genes might drift and eventually differentiate as a new species. One day, then, we will have it in our power to bring a new human species into this world. Whether we choose to follow such a path is for our descendants to decide.

The Borg Route

Even less predictable than our use of genetic manipulation is our manipulation of machines—or they of us. Is the ultimate evolution of our species one of symbiosis with machines, a human-machine synthesis? Many writers have predicted that we might link our bodies with robots or upload our minds into computers. In fact, we are already dependent on machines. As much as we build them to meet human needs, we have structured our own lives and behavior to meet theirs. As machines become ever more complex and interconnected, we will be forced to try to accommodate them. This view was starkly enunciated by George Dyson in his 1998 book *Darwin among the Machines*: "Everything that human beings are doing to make it easier to operate computer networks is at the same time, but for different reasons, making it easier for computer networks to operate human beings.... Darwinian evolution, in one of those paradoxes with which life abounds, may be a victim of its own success, unable to keep up with non-Darwinian processes that it has spawned."

Our technological prowess threatens to swamp the old ways that evolution works. Consider two different views of the future taken from an essay in 2004 by evolutionary philosopher Nick Bostrom of the University of Oxford. On the optimistic side, he wrote: "The big picture shows an overarching trend towards increasing levels of complexity, knowledge, consciousness, and coordinated goal-directed organization, a trend which, not to put too fine a point on it, we may label 'progress.' What we shall call the Panglossian view maintains that this past record of success gives us good grounds for thinking that evolution (whether biological, memetic or technological) will continue to lead in desirable directions."

Although the reference to "progress" surely causes the late evolutionary biologist Steven Jay Gould to spin in his grave, the point can be made. As Gould argued, fossils, including those from our own ancestors, tell us that evolutionary change is not a continuous thing; rather it occurs in fits and starts, and it is certainly not "progressive" or directional. Organisms get smaller as well as larger. But evolution has indeed shown at least one vector: toward increasing complexity. Perhaps that is the fate of future human evolution: greater complexity through some combination of anatomy, physiology or behavior. If we continue to adapt (and undertake some deft planetary engineering), there is no genetic or evolutionary reason that we could not still be around to watch the sun die. Unlike aging, extinction does not appear to be genetically programmed into any species.

The darker side is all too familiar. Bostrom (who must be a very unsettled man) offered a vision of how uploading our brains into computers could spell our doom. Advanced artificial intelligence could encapsulate the various components of human cognition and reassemble those components into something that is no longer human—and that would render us obsolete. Bostrom predicted the following course of events: "Some human individuals upload and make many copies of themselves. Meanwhile, there is gradual progress in neuroscience and artificial intelligence, and eventually it becomes possible to isolate individual cognitive modules and connect them up to modules from other uploaded minds.... Modules that conform to a common standard would be better able to communicate and cooperate with other modules and would therefore be economically more productive, creating a pressure for standardization.... There might be no niche for mental architectures of a human kind."

As if technological obsolescence were not disturbing enough, Bostrom concluded with an even more dreary possibility: if machine efficiency became the new measure of evolutionary fitness, much of what we regard as quintessentially human would be weeded out of our lineage. He wrote: "The extravagancies and fun that arguably give human life much of its meaning—humor, love, game-playing, art, sex, dancing, social conversation, philosophy, literature, scientific discovery, food and drink, friendship, parenting, sport—we have preferences and capabilities that make us engage in such activities, and these predispositions were adaptive in our species' evolutionary past; but what ground do we have for being confident that these or similar activities will continue to be adaptive in the future? Perhaps what will maximize fitness in the future will be nothing but nonstop high-intensity drudgery, work of a drab and repetitive nature, aimed at improving the eighth decimal of some economic output measure."

In short, humanity's future could take one of several routes, assuming we do not go extinct:

- Stasis. We largely stay as we are now, with minor tweaks, mainly as races merge.
- Speciation. A new human species evolves on either this planet or another.
- Symbiosis with machines. Integration of machines and human brains produces a collective intelligence that may or may not retain the qualities we now recognize as human.

Quo vadis Homo futuris?

Evidence Implies That Animals Feel Empathy

By Frans B. M. de Waal

Apart from some rear-guard behaviorists, few people hesitate to ascribe empathy to their dogs. But then dogs are man's best friend, freely credited with lots of human sentiments. For as much as we empathize with our canines, we have been stingy about recognizing empathy elsewhere in the animal kingdom, reserving it as a human trait. This belief is changing, however, as a growing line of research demonstrates not just empathy's existence in other animals but its subtleties and exceptions as well. And they shed some interesting light on how we developed our capacity for caring for others.

Early Studies

The surge in empathy studies during the past decade revives a line of research started more than half a century ago. In 1959 a paper by psychologist Russell Church appeared in the *Journal of Comparative & Physiological Psychology*, provocatively entitled "Emotional Reactions of Rats to the Pain of Others." Church first trained rats to obtain food by pressing a lever. He found that if a rat pressing the lever saw another rat in a neighboring cage receive a shock from an electrified cage floor, the first rat would interrupt its activity—a remarkable result. Why shouldn't the rat continue to get food and simply ignore the other animal's flinching? The bigger question was whether the rats that had stopped pressing the lever were worried about their companions or just afraid that something bad might happen to them as well.

Church's work inspired a brief flurry of research during the 1960s that investigated the presence of "empathy," "sympathy" and "altruism" in animals. To avoid troublesome skepticism from colleagues, the investigators made sure to place the topics of their research in quotation marks; the prevailing behaviorist atmosphere made mention of animal emotions an anathema. Combined with the traditional emphasis on nature's nasty side, this taboo ensured that these studies went largely ignored.

In the meantime, however, human empathy became a respectable study topic. First, in the 1970s, came studies of empathy in young children; then, in the 1980s, in adults. Finally, in the 1990s, researchers began placing humans in brain scanners to monitor them while they watched others who were in pain or distress or who had a disgusted facial expression—revealing many intriguing findings about activity in the brain. This field now produces new articles every week. But for quite some time, animal studies lagged.

An Old Sorrow

This sluggish pace began changing more than a decade ago. Slowly but steadily, some 50 years after Church's rat study, the evolutionary origin of empathy became a hot topic, reviving interest in studies of whether animals experience this complex and socially vital connection to others. Psychologist Stephanie D. Preston of the University of Michigan and I have argued that a basic neural process, first developed in our animal ancestors, underlies even the sophisticated kinds of empathy that only we humans are capable of. Seeing another person in a certain situation reactivates neural representations of when we ourselves have been in similar situations; this brain activity, in turn, generates a body state resembling that of the object of our attention. Thus, to see another's pain may lead us to share it.

This empathetic capacity is in place on the very first day of a person's life. You can see it in any maternity ward, where all newborns will start crying as soon as one of them gets going.

Artificial noise fails to cause the same reaction: babies are particularly sensitive to the distress calls of their own species. I have seen a similar spread of distress in young rhesus monkeys. Once, when an infant monkey had been bitten, it screamed so incessantly that it was soon surrounded by other infants. I counted eight of them climbing on top of the poor victim, pushing, pulling and shoving one another as well as the first infant. The response seemed automatic, as if the other infants were as distraught as the victim was and sought to comfort themselves as much as their companion.

The study of empathy in children started with measures of their reactions to a family member who had been instructed to cry. Very young children would approach and touch or stroke the distressed relative. This reaction became known as empathetic concern.

Now we know that some animals will do the same. Researchers have observed consolation responses in dogs, elephants and primates. After one chimpanzee has attacked another, for example, a bystander will go over to gently embrace the victim until he or she stops yelping.

The tendency to console is so powerful that Nadezhda Ladygina-Kohts (also known as Nadia Kohts), a Russian scientist who raised a juvenile chimpanzee about a century ago, said that if her charge had escaped to the roof of her house there was only one way to get him down. Holding out food would not do the trick: the only way would be for her to sit down and sob, as if she were in pain. The young ape would then rush down from the roof to put an arm around her.

In bonobos, research has shown that empathetic concern is related to emotion regulation. The young bonobos that are best at coping with mental suffering (they scream less if frightened or distressed) are also the first to provide reassurance to others in distress. They are able to comfort others because of their better capacity to tamp down their own emotions. Emotional control is also a major factor in human empathy. There are so many similarities between humans and apes—including the tendency of females to exhibit empathy more readily than males—that the most parsimonious assumption is that the behavior in both species reflects the same mechanism, which may be as old as the mammals.

One of the most rigorous and particularly revealing studies of animal empathy came in 2006 from Dale J. Langford, then a psychology graduate student at McGill University, and her colleagues in a paper entitled "Social Modulation of Pain as Evidence for Empathy in Mice," published June 30, 2006, in *Science*. (Note that this time the word "empathy" is free of quotation marks; this absence reflects the growing consensus that emotional linkage between individuals probably has the same biological origin in humans and other animals.)

This study was inspired by a puzzle that Langford and her laboratory's director, pain geneticist Jeffrey S. Mogil, found intriguing: when they tested mice from the same home cage in experiments that involved light shocks to the feet, the researchers noticed that the order in which the mice were tested seemed to affect their pain response. The first mouse would always show fewer signs of pain than the last. Was the last mouse being sensitized to pain by seeing others in pain? Or was something else at work?

To find out, Langford, Mogil and their colleagues devised an experiment in which pairs of mice were put through a so-called writhing test. In each trial, two mice were placed in two transparent Plexiglas tubes so that they could see each other. Either one or both mice were injected with diluted acetic acid, which is known to cause a mild stomachache. Mice respond to this discomfort with characteristic stretching movements. (This is less a "writhe" than a sort of discomfited restlessness.) The researchers found that an injected mouse would show more of this movement if its partner displayed the same behavior than it would if its partner had not been injected. Most significantly, this increased display occurred only in mouse pairs who were cage mates.

Male (and not female) mice showed an additional interesting phenomenon when witnessing a strange male mouse in pain: its own pain sensitivity would actually drop. This counterempathetic reaction occurred only in male pairs that did not know each other, which are probably the pairs with the greatest degree of rivalry. Was the rivalry suppressing their reaction, or did they feel less empathy for a strange mouse?

(This gender effect reminds me of a wonderful study of human schadenfreude that Tania Singer, then at the University of Zurich, and her colleagues published in early 2006 in *Nature*. The researchers found that in both men and women, seeing the pain of a person with whom one has just cooperated activates pain-related brain areas. But if a man felt he had been treated unfairly by another man in a previous exchange, his brain's pleasure centers would light up at seeing the other's pain. Such male antipathy toward rivals may be a mammalian universal.)

Finally, Langford and her colleagues also exposed pairs of mice to different sources of pain—the acetic acid as before and a radiant heat source that would cause pain if a mouse did not move away. Mice observing a cage mate suffering a stomachache withdrew more quickly from the heat source. In other words, the reactions of mice cannot be attributed to mere imitation, because a mouse seeing a companion in pain appears to be sensitized to *any* pain.

Foundation of Empathy

I admire this study greatly. It is not the kind of manipulation we would nowadays apply to primates, but it goes a long way toward confirming the tentative conclusions of the 1960s, with the benefits of more subjects and more rigorous controls. Although it does not prove that the mice feel vicarious emotions, it demonstrates that they experience a vicarious intensification of their own experience.

This demonstration justifies speaking of "empathy" outside of humanity—at least in some instances. Here we find an interesting division between psychologists, who tend to think in terms of top-down processes, and biologists, who tend to think from the bottom up. The top-down view considers the most advanced forms of empathy, such as putting yourself into another's "shoes" and imagining his or her situation, and wonders how this ability arises; the inevitable answer is advanced cognition, perhaps even language. Yet merely imagining someone else's situation does not constitute empathy. Such imagination can be a cold affair, not unlike understanding how airplanes fly. Empathy requires emotional involvement.

Here the bottom-up view offers a better perspective. When we react to seeing someone display emotion and construct an advanced understanding of the other's situation, this process indeed involves—in humans and in some other large-brained animals—a great deal of cognition. But the emotional connection comes first; understanding and imagination follow. The mouse experiment suggests that the emotional component of this process is at least as old as our early mammalian ancestors and runs deep within us.

The Author Answers Questions

As with most online news columns, Mind Matters at ScientificAmerican.com invites reader comments and questions. Unlike many such columns, however, inquiries often get answered by leading researchers—among them, the authors of posts about recent papers and other scientist visitors to the website—and by *Scientific American* editors. The sampling below includes an exchange between readers and Frans B. M. de Waal. *—The Editors*

> It's always baffled me that any anthropomorphism of animals is considered "unscientific" until the evidence supporting a particular instance is overwhelming. Occam's razor leads one to the opposite point of view. If we accept certain types of behavior as being motivated by particular emotional or mental states in humans, it follows that, barring good evidence to the contrary, the simplest assumption would be that similar behaviors are motivated

by similar internal states in animals. Any argument that can be applied to dismiss this in animals applies equally to humans. Why the false dichotomy? It makes no sense. —*Kevin M.*

Put simply, Occam's razor relates to explanations and states that elements should not be multiplied beyond necessity. Animals being capable of empathy is by far more complex than if they weren't. There is absolutely no reason for us to assume any similarity between our behavior patterns and those of animals. To do so would be in violation of Occam's razor, not the other way around. To save ourselves confusion, it's best to wait for theories like this to be backed up by studies before contemplating what the theories might mean. —*Nick Coad*

DE WAAL REPLIES: It's true that from a cognitive perspective, assuming empathy in animals is not particularly parsimonious. This is usually how Occam's razor is interpreted in psychology. That is a pre-Darwinian interpretation, however. I have argued elsewhere (*Philosophical Topics*, Vol. 27, pages 255–280; 1999) that there is a second kind of parsimony: evolutionary parsimony. This assumes that if two related species act similarly under similar circumstances, the simplest assumption is that the psychology behind their behavior is similar, too. The alternative would be to assume the separate evolution of similar behavior, which is not particularly elegant or economic. So, take your pick! I personally opt for the Darwinian version of Occam's razor.

Referenced

"Empathy: Its Ultimate and Proximate Bases." Stephanie D. Preston and Frans B. M. de Waal in *Behavioral and Brain Sciences*, Vol. 25, No. 1, pages 1–20; 2002.

"Grasping the Intentions of Others with One's Own Mirror Neuron System." Marco Iacoboni, Istvan Molnar-Szakacs, Vittorio Gallese, Giovanni Buccino, John C. Mazziotta and Giacomo Rizzolatti in *PLOS Biology*, Vol. 3, No. 3, pages 529–535; March 2005. Published online February 22, 2005.

"Empathetic Neural Responses Are Modulated by the Perceived Fairness of Others." Tania Singer, Ben Seymour, John P. O'Doherty, Klaas E. Stephan, Raymond J. Dolan and Chris D. Frith in *Nature*, Vol. 439, pages 466–469; January 26, 2006.

"Putting the Altruism Back into Altruism: The Evolution of Empathy." Frans B. M. de

Waal in *Annual Review of Psychology*, Vol. 59, pages 279–300; 2008.

About the Author

Frans B. M. de Waal is director of the Living Links Center at Emory University, where he studies the behavior and evolution of primates. He is author of The Age of Empathy: Nature's Lessons for a Kinder Society *(Harmony Books, 2009).*

The Search for Extraterrestrial Life as We Don't Know It

By Sarah Scoles

Sarah Stewart Johnson was a college sophomore when she first stood atop Hawaii's Mauna Kea volcano. Its dried lava surface was so different from the eroded, tree-draped mountains of her home state of Kentucky. Johnson wandered away from the other young researchers she was with and toward a distant ridge of the 13,800-foot summit. Looking down, she turned over a rock with the toe of her boot. To her surprise, a tiny fern lived underneath it, having sprouted from ash and cinder cones. "It felt like it stood for all of us, huddled under that rock, existing against the odds," Johnson says.

Her true epiphany, though, wasn't about the hardiness of life on Earth or the hardships of being human: It was about aliens. Even if a landscape seemed strange and harsh from a human perspective, other kinds of life might find it quite comfortable. The thought opened up the cosmic real estate, and the variety of life, she imagined might be beyond Earth's atmosphere. "It was on that trip that the idea of looking for life in the universe began to make sense to me," Johnson says.

Later, Johnson became a professional at looking. As an astronomy postdoc at Harvard University in the late 2000s and early 2010s she investigated how astronomers might use genetic sequencing—detecting and identifying DNA and RNA—to find evidence of aliens. Johnson found the work exciting (the future alien genome project!), but it also made her wonder: What if extraterrestrial life didn't have DNA or RNA or other nucleic acids? What if their cells got instructions in some other biochemical way?

As an outlet for heretical thoughts like this, Johnson started writing in a style too lyrical and philosophical for scientific journals. Her typed musings would later turn into the 2020 popular science book *The Sirens of Mars*. Inside its pages, she probed the idea that other planets were truly other, and so their inhabitants might be very different, at a fundamental and chemical level, from anything on this world. "Even places that seem familiar—like Mars, a place that we think we know intimately—can completely throw us for a loop," she says. "What if that's the case for life?"

If Johnson's musings are correct, the current focus of the hunt for aliens—searching for life as we know it—might not work for finding biology in the beyond. "There's this old maxim that if you lose your keys at night, the first place you look is under the lamppost," says Johnson, who is now an associate professor at Georgetown University. If you want to find life, look first at the only way you know life can exist: in places kind of like Earth, with chemistry kind of like Earthlings'.

Much of astrobiology research involves searching for chemical "biosignatures"—molecules or combinations of molecules that could indicate the presence of life. But because scientists can't reliably say that ET life should look, chemically, like Earth life, seeking those signatures could mean we miss beings that might be staring us in the face. "How do we move beyond that?" Johnson asks. "How do we contend with the truly alien?" Scientific methods, she thought, should be more open to varieties of life based on varied biochemistry: life as we don't know it. Or, in a new term coined here, "LAWDKI."

Now Johnson is getting a chance to figure out how, exactly, to contend with that unknown kind of life, as the principal investigator of a new NASA-funded initiative called the Laboratory for Agnostic Biosignatures (LAB). LAB's research doesn't count on ET having specific biochemistry at all, so it doesn't look for specific biosignatures. LAB aims to find more fundamental markers of biology, such as evidence of complexity—intricately arranged molecules that are unlikely to assemble themselves without some kind of biological forcing—and disequilibrium, such as unexpected concentrations of molecules on other planets or moons. These are proxies for life as no one knows it.

Maybe someday, if LAB has its way, they will become more than proxies. These signals could help answer one of humankind's oldest questions—Are we alone?—and show us that we're not so special, and neither is our makeup.

Life, Astro Life or Lyfe

Part of the difficulty in searching for life of any sort is that scientists don't agree on how life started in the first place—or what life even *is*. One good attempt at a definition came in 2011 from geneticist Edward Trifonov, who collated more than 100 interpretations of the word "life" and distilled them into one overarching idea: it's "self-reproduction with variations." NASA formulated a similar working definition years earlier, in the mid-1990s, and still uses it to design astrobiology studies. Life, according to this formulation, "is a self-sustaining chemical system capable of Darwinian evolution."

Neither of those classical definitions requires a particular chemistry. On Earth, of course, life runs on DNA: deoxyribonucleic acid. DNA is made up of two twisted strands, each comprising alternating sugar and phosphate groups. Stuck to every sugar is a base—the As (adenine), Gs (guanine), Cs (cytosine), and Ts (thymine). Together the bases and sugar-phosphates form nucleotides; DNA itself is a nucleic acid. RNA is kind of like single-stranded DNA—among other things, it helps translate DNA's instructions into actual protein production.

The simple letters in a genetic sequence, strung together in a laddered order, carry all the information needed to make you, squirrels and sea anemones. DNA can replicate, and DNA from different organisms (when they really, really love one another) can mix and meld to form a new organism that can replicate itself in turn. If biology elsewhere relied on this same chemistry, it would be life as we know it.

Scientists assume all forms of life would need some way to pass down biological instructions whose shifts could also help the species evolve over time. But it's conceivable that aliens might not make these instructions out of the same chemicals as ours—or in the same shape. For instance, starting in the 1990s, Northwestern University researchers made SNAs, spherical nucleic acids.

Alien life could have genetic code with, say, different bases. NASA-supported 2019 research, from the Foundation for Applied Molecular Evolution, successfully created synthetic DNA that used the four old-school bases and four new ones: P, Z, B and S. Scientists have also altered the strand part of genetic code, creating XNA—where X means anything goes—that uses a molecule such as cyclohexene (CeNA) or glycol (GNA), rather than deoxyribose. Big thinkers have long suggested that rather than using carbon as a base, as all these molecules do, perhaps alien life might use the functionally similar element silicon—meaning it wouldn't have nucleic acids at all but other molecules that perhaps play the same role. If we can whip up such diversity in our minds and our labs, shouldn't the universe be even more creative and capable?

It's for that reason that LAB collaborator Leroy Cronin of the University of Glasgow doesn't think scientists should even be talking about *biology* off-Earth at all. "Biology is unique," he proclaims. RNA, DNA, proteins, typical amino acids? "Only going to be found on Earth." He thinks someday people will instead say, "We're looking for 'astro life.'" (LAWDKI has yet to catch on.)

Stuart Bartlett, a researcher at the California Institute of Technology and unaffiliated with LAB, agrees with the linguistic critique. The search for weird life isn't actually a search for life, Bartlett argues. It's a search for "lyfe," a term proposed in a 2020 article he co-authored in, ironically, the journal *Life*. "Lyfe," the paper says, "is defined as any system that fulfills all four processes of the living state." That means that it dissipates energy (by, say, eating and digesting), uses self-sustaining chemical reactions to make exponentially more of itself, maintains its internal conditions as external conditions change, and takes in information about the environment that it then uses to survive. "Life," meanwhile, the paper continues, "is defined as the instance of lyfe that we are familiar with on Earth."

Bartlett's work, though separate from LAB's, emerges from the same fascination: "That mysterious, opaque transition between things like physics and chemistry that we understand fairly well," he says, "and then biology that is still shrouded in mystery." How life becomes life at all is perhaps the most central question of astrobiology.

Trying to figure out how biology emerged on the planet we know best is the province of "origin of life" studies. There are two main hypotheses for how clumps of chemistry became lumps of biology—a process called abiogenesis. One holds that RNA arose able to make more of itself, because that's what it does, and that it could also catalyze other chemical reactions. Over time that replication led to beings whose makeup relied on that genetic code. The "metabolism-first" framework, on the other hand, posits that chemical reactions organized in a self-sustaining way. Those compound communities and their chemical reactions grew more complex and eventually spit out genetic code.

Those two main hypotheses aren't mutually exclusive. John Sutherland, a chemist at the Medical Research Council Laboratory of Molecular Biology, is co-director of a group called the Simons Collaboration on the Origins of Life, which merges previous ideas about how one or another subsystem, such as genetics or early metabolism, came first. But if he's being real, Sutherland admits he doesn't understand how biology got started. No one does.

And until scientists know more about how things probably went down on the early Earth, Sutherland argues, there's no way to estimate how common extraterrestrial anything might be. It doesn't matter that there are trillions of stars in billions of galaxies: If the events that led to life are supremely uncommon, those many solar systems might still not be enough, statistically, to have resulted in abiogenesis—in other beings.

Bio-Agnostic

The first issue of the academic journal *Astrobiology*, more than two decades ago, featured an article by Kenneth Nealson and Pamela

Section 1: Life and Evolution

Conrad called "A Non-Earth-centric Approach to Life Detection." But taking a non-Earth-centric approach isn't easy for our brains, which formed in this environment. We are notoriously bad at picturing the unfamiliar. "It's one of the biggest challenges we have, like imagining a color we've never seen," Johnson says.

So astrobiologists often end up looking for aliens that resemble Earth life. Astronomers like to consider oxygen in an exoplanet atmosphere as a potential indicator of life—because we breathe it—although a planet can fill up with that gas in less lively ways. On Mars, researchers have been psyched by puffs of methane, organic molecules, and the release of gas after soil was fed a solution of what we on Earth call nutrients, perhaps indicating metabolism. They create terms like "the Goldilocks zone" for the regions around stars where planets could host liquid water, implying that what's just right for Earth life is also just right everywhere else.

Even when scientists do discover biology unfamiliar to them, they tend to relate it to something familiar. For instance, when Antonie van Leeuwenhoek saw single-celled organisms through his microscope's compound lens in the 17th century, he dubbed them "animalcules," or little animals, which they are not.

Heather Graham, who works at NASA's Goddard Space Flight Center and is LAB's deputy principal investigator, sees van Leeuwenhoek's discovery as a successful search for LAWDKI, close to home. The same description applies to scientists' discovery of Archaea, a domain of ancient single-celled organisms first recognized in the 1970s. "If you reframe those discoveries as agnostic biosignatures in action, you realize that people have been doing this for a while," Graham says.

Around 2016, Johnson joined their ranks, finding some like-minded nonbelievers who wanted to probe that darkness. At an invitation-only NASA workshop about biosignatures, Johnson sat at a table with scientists like Graham, gaming out how they might use complexity as a proxy for biology. On an exaggerated macroscale, the idea is that if you come across a fleet of 747s on Mars, you might not know where they came from, but you know they're unlikely to be random. Someone, or something, created them.

After the meeting, Johnson and her co-conspirators put in a last-minute proposal to develop an instrument for NASA. It would find and measure molecules whose shapes fit physically together like lock and key because that rarely happens in random collections of chemical compounds but pops up all over living cells. The instrument idea, though, didn't make the cut. "That's when we realized, 'Okay, we need to roll this back and do a lot more fundamental work,'" Graham says.

The space agency would give them a chance to do so, soon putting out a call for "Interdisciplinary Consortia for Astrobiology Research." It promised multiple years of funding to dig deeper into Johnson and her associates' lunch-table ideas. They needed a larger team, though, so they pinged planetary scientists, biologists, chemists, computer scientists, mathematicians and engineers—some space-centric to the core and others, Johnson says, "just beginning to consider the astrobiology implications of their work." It was particularly important to do this now because researchers are planning to send life-detection instruments to destinations such as the solar system moons Europa, Enceladus and Titan, more exotic than most of the worlds visited so far. "Most of these other places we're beginning to think about as targets for astrobiology are really weird and different," Johnson says. If you're going to a weird and different place, you might expect weird and different life, squirming invisibly beyond the reach of a lamppost's light.

Their pitch worked: The expanded lunch table became LAB. Now the project, a spread-out coalition of scientists more than a single physical laboratory, is a few years deep into its work. The researchers aim to learn how things like the complexity of a surface, anomalous concentrations of elements and energy transfer—such as the movement of electrons between atoms—might reveal life as no one knows it.

LAB Work

LAB's research is a combination of fieldwork, lab projects and computation. One project is a planned visit to Canada's Kidd Creek Mine, which drops nearly 10,000 feet into the ground. Its open pit looks like a quarry reaching toward the seventh circle of hell. At those depths, around 2.7 billion years ago, an ocean floor brewed with volcanic activity, which left sulfide ore behind. The conditions are similar(ish) to what astronomers believe they might find on an "ocean world" like Europa. In the mine, the scientists hope to probe the differences between minerals that formed by crystallization—when atoms fall out of solution and into an ordered, lattice structure in the same place they are now—and evidence of biology.

The two kinds of materials can look superficially alike because they're both highly ordered. But the team aims to show that geochemical models, which simulate how water saturated with chemicals will precipitate them out, will predict the kind of abiotic crystals found there. Kidd Creek, for instance, has its own sort: Kiddcreekite, a combination of the copper, tin, tungsten and sulfur that crystallizes from the water. Those same models, however, aren't likely to predict biological structures, which form according to different forces and rules. If that turns out to be true, the models may prove useful when applied to alien geochemical conditions to predict the naturally forming minerals. Anything else that's found there, the thinking goes, might be alive.

Johnson is reaching back to her postdoc days, using the genetic sequencers whose relevance she called into question back then. The group, though, has found a way to make them more agnostic. The researchers plan to use the instruments to investigate the number of spots on a cell's surface where molecules can attach themselves—like the places where antibodies stick to cells. "We had this hypothesis that there are more binding sites on something complicated like a cell than a small particle," Johnson says, such as an unalive mote of dust. Something alive, in other words, should have more lock-and-key places.

To test this idea, they create a random pool of DNA snippets and send it toward a cell. Some snippets will hook up with the cell's exterior. The scientists next remove and collect the bound snippets, then capture the unbound snippets and send them back to the target cell again, repeating the process for several cycles. Then they see what's left at the end—how much has hooked on and how much is still free. In this way, the researchers can compare the keys locked into the cell with those attached to something like a dust particle.

The scientists will also scrutinize another key difference they suspect divides life and not-life: Things that are not alive tend to be at a kind of equilibrium with their environment. In contrast, something that's alive will harness energy to maintain a difference from its surroundings, LAB member Peter Girguis of Harvard hypothesizes. "It's using power to keep ourselves literally separate from the environment, defining our boundary," he says. Take this example: When a branch is part of a tree, it's alive, and it's different—in a bordered way—from its environment. If you remove that life from its energy source—pluck the branch—it dies and stops using power. "In a matter of time, it disintegrates and becomes indistinguishable from the environment," Girguis says. "In other words, it literally goes to equilibrium."

The disequilibrium of living should show up as a *chemical* difference between an organism and its surroundings—regardless of what the surroundings, or the life, are made of. "I can go scan something, make a map and say, 'Show me the distribution of potassium,'" Girguis says. If blobs of concentrated K appear, dotting the cartography only in certain spots, you may have biology on your hands.

Girguis's LAB work intertwines with another pillar of the group's research: a concept called chemical fractionation, which is how life preferentially uses some elements and isotopes and ignores others. A subgroup investigating this idea, led by Christopher House of Pennsylvania State University, can use the usual data that space instruments take to suss out the makeup of a planet or moon. "If you understand the fundamental rules about the inclusion or exclusion of elements and isotopes, then you can imagine a different ecosystem where it still behaves by similar rules, but the elements and isotopes are totally different," House says. It could give disequilibrium researchers a starting point for which kinds of patterns to focus on when making their dotted maps.

Within House's group, postdoc researchers are studying sediments left by ancient organisms in Western Australia. Looking at these rock samples, they try to capture patterns showing which elements or isotopes early Earth life was picky about. "We're hopeful that we can start to generalize," House says.

LAB's computing team, co-led by Chris Kempes of the Santa Fe Institute, is all about such generalizing. Kempes's research focuses on a concept called scaling—in this case, how the chemistry inside a cell changes predictably with its size and how the abundance of different-sized cells follows a particular pattern. With LAB, Kempes, House, Graham and their collaborators published a paper in 2021 in the *Bulletin of Mathematical Biology* about how scaling laws would apply to bacteria. For instance, if you sort a sample of biological material by size, differences pop out. Small cells' chemistry looks a lot like their environment's. "The bigger cells will be more and more different from the environment," Kempes says.

The abundance of cells of different sizes tends to follow a relationship known as a power law: Lots of small things with a steep drop-off as cells get larger. If you took an extraterrestrial sample, then, and saw those mathematical relationships play out—small things that looked like their surroundings, with progressively larger things looking less like their environments, with lots of the former and few of the latter—that might indicate a biological system. And you wouldn't need to know ahead of time what either "environment" or "biology" looked like chemically.

Cronin, a sort of heretic within this heretic group, has his own idea for differentiating between living and not. He's an originator of something called assembly theory, a "way of identifying if something is complex without knowing anything about its origin," he says.

The more complex a molecule is, the more likely it is to have come from a living process.

That can sound like a bias in the agnosticism, but everyone generally concedes that life results from, as Sutherland puts it, "the complexification of matter." In the beginning, there was the big bang. Hydrogen, the simplest element, formed. Then came helium. Much later there were organic molecules—conglomerations of carbon atoms with other elements attached. Those organic molecules eventually came together to form a self-sustaining, self-replicating system. Eventually that system started to build the biological equivalent of 747s (and then actual 747s).

In assembly theory, the complexity of molecules can be quantified by their "molecular assembly number." It's just an integer indicating how many building blocks are required to bond together, and in what quantities, to make a molecule. The group uses the word "abracadabra" (magic!) as an example. To make that magic, you first need to add an *a* and a *b*. To that *ab*, you can add *r*. To *abr*, toss in another *a* to make *abra*. Then attach a *c*, then an *a* and then a *d*, and you get *abracad*. And to *abracad*, you can add the *abra* that you've already made. That's seven steps to make *abracadabra*, whose molecular assembly number is thus seven. The group postulated that a higher number meant a molecule would have a more complicated "fingerprint" on a mass spectrometer—a tool that separates a sample's components by their mass and charge to identify what it's made of. A complex molecule would show more distinct peaks of energy, in part because it was made of many bonds. And those peaks are a rough proxy for its assembly number.

Cronin had bragged that by doing mass spectrometry, he could measure the complexity of a molecule without even knowing what the molecule was. If the technique indicated that a molecule's complexity crossed a given threshold, it probably came from a biological process.

Still, he needed to prove it. Through LAB, NASA gave him double-blind samples of material to yea or nay as biological. The material hailed from outer space, fossil beds and the sediments of bays, among other places. One of the samples was from the Murchison meteorite, a 220-pound hunk of rock, full of organic compounds. "They thought the technique would fail because Murchison is probably one of the most complex interstellar materials," he says. But it succeeded: "It basically says Murchison seems a bit weird, but it's dead."

Another sample contained 14-million-year-old fossils, sculpted by biology but meant to fool the method into a "dead" hit because of their age. "The technique found that they were of living origin pretty easily," Cronin says. His results appeared in *Nature Communications* in 2021 and helped to convince Cronin's colleagues that his line of research was worthy. "There are a lot of skeptical people in [LAB's] team, actually," he says.

Aliens Discovered??

There is plenty of skepticism outside LAB as well. Some scientists question the need to search for unfamiliar life when we still haven't done much searching for extraterrestrial life as we know it. "I think there's still a lot we can explore before we go to life as we don't know it," says Martina Preiner of the Royal Netherlands Institute for Sea Research and Utrecht University.

Still, even among old-school astrobiology researchers looking for Earth-like signatures on exoplanets, the LAB approach has support. Victoria Meadows of the University of Washington has been thinking about such far-off signals for two decades. She's seen the field change over that time—complexify, if you will. Scientists have gone from thinking "if you see oxygen on a planet, slam dunk," to thinking "there are no slam dunks." "I think what my team has helped provide and how the field has evolved is this understanding that biosignatures must be interpreted in the context of their environment," she says. You have to understand a planet's conditions, and those of its star, well enough to figure out what oxygen might *mean*. "It may be that the environment itself can either back up your idea that oxygen is due to life or potentially that the environment itself may produce a false positive," she says, such as from an ocean boiling off.

In a lot of ways, Meadows says, looking for agnostic biosignatures is the ultimate way to take such cosmic conditions into account. "You have to understand the environment exquisitely to be able to tell that something anomalous—something that isn't a planetary process—is operating in that environment," she says. Still, this variety of alien hunting is in its infancy. "I think they're really just starting off," she says. "I think what LAB is doing in particular is a pioneering effort on really getting some science under this concept."

Even so, Meadows isn't sure how likely LAWDKI is. "The question is, 'Is the environment on a [terrestrial] extrasolar planet going to be so different that the solutions are so different?'" Meadows asks. If the conditions are similar and the chemicals are similar, it's reasonable to think life itself will be similar. "We are expecting to see some similar science if these environments are similar, but of course I will expect that there'll be things that will surprise us as well." It's for all these reasons that Meadows, whose work focuses on exoplanets, is working with the LAB scientists, whose research for now homes in on the solar system, to bring their two worlds together.

By the end of LAB's grant, the team plans to develop instruments that will help spacecraft notice weird and different life close to home. "We're extremely focused on the ultimate goal—how we can take these tools and techniques and help develop them to the point they can become instruments on space missions," Johnson says.

No one piece of information, gathered from a single instrument, can reliably label something life, though. So the group is working toward suites of devices, drawing on all their focus areas, that work together in different environments, such as worlds wrapped in liquid versus rocky deserts. Graham is gathering sample sets that LAB's subgroups can test in a round-robin way to see how the superimposition of their results stacks up. They might look for, say, molecules with big assembly numbers concentrated in bounded areas that look different from their environment.

Even if these approaches collectively find something, it's unlikely to provide a definitive answer to the question "Are we alone?" It will probably yield a "maybe," at least for a while. That grayness may disappoint those who'd like "Aliens discovered!" headlines, instead of "Aliens discovered?? Check back in 10 years."

"I understand that frustration," Johnson says, "because I'm a restless sort of person." That restlessness relates in part to her own mortality. The end of the time when she's out of equilibrium with her environment. The demise of her complexity, of her detectability and ability to detect. "We have these ephemeral lives," she says. "We have this world that's going to end. We have this star that's going to die. We have this incredible moment. Here we are: alive and sentient beings on this planet." All because, at some point, life *started*.

That may have happened tens or hundreds or thousands or millions or billions of other times on other planets. Or, maybe, it has only happened here. "It just feels," Johnson says, "like an extraordinary thing that I want to know about the universe before I die."

About the Author

Sarah Scoles is a Colorado-based science journalist, a contributing editor at Scientific American *and a senior contributor at* Undark. *Her newest book is* Countdown: The Blinding Future of Nuclear Weapons *(Bold Type Books, 2024).*

Section 2: Physics Mysteries

2.1　The Weirdest Particles in the Universe
　　　By Clara Moskowitz
2.2　Why Aren't We Made of Antimatter?
　　　By Luke Caldwell
2.3　Something Is Wrong with Dark Energy, Physicists Say
　　　By Rebecca Boyle

The Weirdest Particles in the Universe

By Clara Moskowitz

They're small, nearly imperceptible, and there are 500 trillion of them passing through you right now. Neutrinos are among nature's most plentiful yet mysterious creations. Science writer James Riordon recently set out to list what was known versus unknown about neutrinos, and he found the second column was longer. "To me, the most interesting thing is how we know surprisingly little about them," he says. "These are definitely here and definitely mysterious. The exciting science lies in answering these questions."

In the new book *Ghost Particle: In Search of the Elusive and Mysterious Neutrino* (MIT Press, 2023), Riordon and his co-author, physicist Alan Chodos, document how the surprising particles were first proposed and discovered and what scientists have figured out so far—plus everything they hope to eventually understand. Because of their many oddities, neutrinos seem like promising conduits for answering some of our biggest questions: Why is the universe made of matter and not antimatter? What is dark matter? And can anything travel faster than light?

Scientific American spoke to Riordon about why these bizarre bits of nature are so cool and how his own family history fits into the story of neutrinos.

[An edited transcript of the interview follows.]

Q: So you actually have a personal connection to neutrinos. What is it?
A: I am the grandson of one of the co-discoverers of neutrinos, Clyde Cowan, Jr. But he passed away when I was nine. There was always a mythology in my family about him, but it wasn't really clear what he had done. It wasn't something I understood until I went to study physics in college. My interest developed

more as I became a science writer and started seeing these interesting neutrino results coming out.

I talked to MIT Press about doing a book, and they were interested, but they wanted to make sure there was an expert in the field writing with me. I thought of Alan Chodos, a theoretician who thinks outside the box. He has written some interesting speculations about neutrinos that are a little bit on the edge.

Q: Which of the myriad of questions neutrinos pose intrigues you the most?
A: My favorite mystery is the determination of whether or not it's its own antiparticle. To me, I think that's the biggest and most dramatic question about neutrinos. That one touches on the really big question of the origin of the universe.

If a neutrino does turn out to be its own antiparticle, it could allow us to understand why the universe is made of mostly matter and not antimatter. We know that when the universe first began, it had to be a perfect balance of matter and antimatter. There'd be no matter left if all the matter and the antimatter in the universe had just annihilated. So an imbalance had to arrive somewhere, and neutrinos could be a clue as to the source of that imbalance.

Q: You write, "The very idea of neutrinos was a terrible thing, in the words of the first person who imagined it." Wolfgang Pauli proposed neutrinos in 1930 to explain why there seemed to be missing energy and momentum in a certain type of particle decay. Why was the neutrino solution so terrible?
A: It almost seemed like a sleight of hand. They had a problem with beta decay, this nuclear reaction that seemed to have something missing. So to sit and say, "What's missing? Let's just scrape all those things that are missing and put them together into a new particle" to answer the question, it feels like a "just-so story"—like "How did Leopard get its spots? Well, some ancient

god threw mud at him." Sure, it's *an* answer. But you can't check it. It solves your problem, but it's unsatisfying.

Q: Pauli assumed he couldn't check the answer because he and other physicists thought neutrinos would be completely undetectable. Yet we've now seen three different types of them. And is there a chance there are even more?

A: At Los Alamos [National Laboratory in New Mexico], they were finding there were too many neutrinos turning up in one of their experiments. One explanation would be that there is yet another type of neutrino that only interacts with other neutrinos and perhaps some sort of dark matter. Those are called sterile neutrinos. There's reason to believe that there may be many types of neutrinos, but that's just a possibility.

People expected this Los Alamos anomaly to go away. They were testing it at other machines at [Fermi National Accelerator Laboratory in Illinois]. I remember talking to the people at Los Alamos who had first found what appeared to be the suggestive sterile neutrinos, and they all expected there to be absolutely no sign of sterile neutrinos [from the follow-up test]. Instead it confirmed their initial experiment that suggested there were sterile neutrinos. It was a stunning confirmation of something that almost everybody assumed was just a measurement error. The question is still clearly out there, and there are reasons to believe both sides: that there's some kind of systematic error that both are subject to *or* that the question's still out. That hopefully will be answered soon.

Q: Another big mystery is what neutrinos actually weigh. At first, they were predicted to be massless, but now scientists know they must have nonzero mass. Where do we stand on figuring out what that mass is?

A: One of the things that's really fun to talk to Alan about is that KATRIN [a German experiment aiming to measure neutrinos' mass] doesn't say the neutrinos have a small positive mass. It says they have a small mass that could be either positive or negative mass squared. That means they could have, based on the way they do the experiment, an imaginary mass, which would make them "tachyonic neutrinos." This would make them potentially travel faster than the speed of light or potentially backward in time, depending on how you think about it.

Of course, the people at KATRIN don't believe that that's a possibility, so they just throw that away. But there's still this slight hope in the minds of people such as Alan that maybe the answer will actually be negative, even though they're just including it to make sure their statistics don't get screwed up.

Q: If neutrinos could travel faster than light, wouldn't we know that already?
A: It's true there would be all kinds of problems. I spoke to [physicist] Sheldon Glashow and asked him about that. He pointed out that if neutrinos could travel faster than light, it would lead to a huge burst of radiation, and they would rapidly slow down. So even if they could momentarily travel faster than the speed of light, they would instantly not travel faster than light. I tend to believe in Sheldon Glashow's answer. Alan holds out hope because he's a theoretician, and they like to believe weird stuff. It's not something that anyone, even Alan, seriously expects to see.

Q: After doing all this research and writing this book, did it change how you feel about your grandfather?
A: It did. I found that there's a huge amount of humor in what he and Fred Reines [his collaborator on the neutrino discovery experiments] did. They had the audacity to encode a little joke into the design of a tremendous scientific experiment.

Q: Their first idea to look for neutrinos was to take advantage of the nuclear weapons testing being done during the Manhattan Project at Los Alamos, right?

A: If you look at the initial proposal, which was in itself audacious, they were going to put a detector in a shaft and drop it at the same time that a nuclear weapon went off about 40 meters away. It was an incredibly complicated system to develop. They had to decide where to dig the shaft. And they chose to put it 137 feet away from the tower where the weapon was going to go off. They chose that because the fine structure constant [a fundamental constant related to the strength of the electromagnetic force] is $1/137$. But they knew that that was a little too frivolous to put in the description of the experiment for approval by Los Alamos, so they found the metric equivalent, which was roughly 40 meters. They turned it into an inside joke.

Then when they had the experiment that actually discovered the neutrino, in South Carolina, they put up all this shielding to see if they could modulate the signal and, along with the shielding, one pound of hominy grits. I think I romanticize my grandfather as this funny guy, and it became fleshed out. You can see this sense of humor and this sense of fun that went through this very serious activity they were doing.

About the Author

Clara Moskowitz is a senior editor at Scientific American, *where she covers astronomy, space, physics and mathematics. She has been at Scientific American for a decade; previously she worked at Space.com. Moskowitz has reported live from rocket launches, space shuttle liftoffs and landings, suborbital spaceflight training, mountaintop observatories, and more. She has a bachelor's degree in astronomy and physics from Wesleyan University and a graduate degree in science communication from the University of California, Santa Cruz.*

Why Aren't We Made of Antimatter?

By Luke Caldwell

The universe shouldn't be here. Everything scientists know about particle physics, summed up in a theory called the Standard Model, suggests that the big bang should have created equal quantities of matter and antimatter. A mirror version of matter, antimatter consists of partner particles for all the regular particles we know of, equal in every way but with opposite charge. When matter and antimatter particles collide, they destroy one another, so the mass created when the universe was born should have been completely wiped out, leaving an empty, featureless cosmos containing only light. That there was enough leftover matter after this great annihilation to form galaxies, stars, planets and even us but almost no antimatter is known as the matter-antimatter imbalance. This existential anomaly is one of the great outstanding mysteries of modern physics.

Physicists have concocted many hypotheses to explain this mismatch, but we don't know which, if any, are true. Some of them seek to offer matter the upper hand by introducing new particles that decay, producing more matter than antimatter in the process, or that interact differently with matter and antimatter. And some of these proposals include side effects that scientists can hope to detect, thereby providing evidence for the theories. One example is an exotic property of electrons called the electric dipole moment, a small difference between the center of mass of an electron and its center of charge. Such a displacement has never been detected and should be much smaller than current experiments could measure. But many proposed extensions to the Standard Model that seek to explain the matter-antimatter imbalance predict much larger values for the electric dipole moment.

Recently I worked with colleagues to attempt to detect this signal. Our laboratory, nestled against the foothills of the Rocky Mountains at JILA, a research institute of the University of Colorado Boulder, took a different route than usual experiments. We pioneered a new strategy that allowed us to make the most precise measurement yet of the electric dipole moment.

To understand what we were looking for, imagine any simple physics experiment. Now picture repeating that experiment with all positive charges replaced by negative ones (and vice versa) and the entire apparatus arranged in the opposite direction as if reflected in a mirror. If you got an equivalent result with the mirror setup, the experiment would be said to conserve charge and parity symmetry (CP symmetry for short). In 1967 physicist Andrei Sakharov showed that this symmetry is intimately connected to the matter-antimatter imbalance. If our universe as we currently find it developed from a universe that was initially composed of equal parts matter and antimatter, something must have happened to break CP symmetry, Sakharov found. Around the same time, other researchers discovered that nature does sometimes violate CP symmetry. For instance, the weak force—responsible for radioactivity in atomic nuclei—slightly breaks this symmetry when it interacts with quarks. Yet the instances of known CP violation in the Standard Model aren't enough to explain the matter-antimatter imbalance. We must find new, undiscovered physics phenomena that don't conserve CP symmetry to solve the mystery.

That's where our experiment comes in. It searches for evidence of new particles in the universe by looking for subtle effects on known particles. These effects occur because of the nature of the Standard Model, which is a type of quantum field theory. In quantum field theories, the basic building blocks of the universe are fields, not particles. There is a field for each of the particles in nature, from common particles such as electrons and photons to their more exotic cousins such as muons and gluons. You can imagine two-dimensional analogues of these fields as huge, flexible sheets that extend through all of space, supporting ripples like the surface of a lake does. In a quantum field, ripples can occur only in certain discrete sizes. The smallest possible ripple in a given field is what we call a particle; positive ripples in the field are matter particles, and negative ripples in the field are antimatter particles.

The amount of energy it takes to create the smallest possible ripple depends on the stiffness of the stretchy sheet; this minimum amount of energy is the rest mass of the associated particle. The different fields are linked together—or "coupled"—so that a ripple in one field disturbs the connected fields. For example, an oscillating ripple in the electron field creates accompanying ripples in the electromagnetic field corresponding to photons, a phenomenon we make good use of in everyday devices such as radio antennae and mobile phones.

Physicists' most successful tools for discovering new fields, and the particles associated with them, have historically been particle colliders. These machines direct two particles—protons, for example—to fly toward each other at high speeds. When the particles (ripples) crash into each other like two water waves meeting on a beach, their violent interactions can cause some of their energy to be carried off as ripples in other fields. If the energy of their collision is exactly equal to the energy needed to create a ripple in one of the other fields they are coupled to, we get what's called resonant enhancement, which greatly increases the probability of a new particle being created. Such collision resonances were used to discover many of the fields we know about—including the most recently confirmed piece of the Standard Model, the Higgs field, with its associated particle, the Higgs boson.

The world's most powerful accelerator, the 27-kilometer ring of the Large Hadron Collider (LHC) near Geneva, is now operating at the highest collision energies it was designed for, but so far it hasn't discovered any other new fields. If undiscovered fields exist, either their mass is higher than the LHC can reach or their coupling to the fields of the Standard Model is too weak for the LHC to create them. A new particle collider capable of reaching much higher energies is likely to cost many tens of billions of dollars, and as a result, even agreeing on whether and how it should be funded is likely to take many years.

Luckily, there is another way to detect new particles and fields, which involves making precision measurements. As mentioned earlier, because the fields of the Standard Model are coupled, a ripple corresponding to a particle in one field always causes disturbances in other fields. For example, an electron—a ripple in the electron field—disturbs the electromagnetic field around it. This disturbance in the electromagnetic field in turn disturbs the other fields that are coupled to it, and so on, eventually including all known fields of the Standard Model. What we call an electron is actually a composite excitation of all these fields, like a large water wave causing disturbances in the air above it. The effect is sometimes referred to as the electron being surrounded by a cloud of "virtual particles."

These accompanying disturbances of the other fields affect many of the electron's properties, so by carefully measuring these properties, we can infer the presence of any undiscovered fields that are coupled to the electron. If those fields are associated with heavier particles, they are stiffer and therefore less disturbed by the rippling electron field—meaning they cause less of a change to the electron's properties. Measuring the effects of fields with particles of higher and higher masses thus requires measurements with greater and greater precision.

One difficulty of this approach is that often the kind of change we're looking for is overshadowed by modifications from fields of the Standard Model. For example, an electron has a magnetic field similar to a tiny bar magnet. The strength of this field is the electron's magnetic dipole moment, and it has been measured to very high precision. Its value is determined mostly by the magnetic moment of the bare electron field; the largest changes arise from the electromagnetic field, and they can be calculated with astonishing precision. At the level of precision achieved by current experiments, however, the exact value of the Standard Model coupling between an electron and electromagnetic fields is not exactly known—there is some discrepancy in the measured values from different experiments. Even if this problem is resolved, the tiny effects of interactions with quark fields and the strong force will be important. These effects can be incredibly complex and difficult to calculate, making our search for similar-sized (or smaller) effects from exotic physics challenging.

A nice way around this problem is to find a property that is zero (or very, very small) in the Standard Model. According to the theory, there should be only a minuscule separation between an electron's center of mass and center of charge—in other words, its electric dipole moment. The electric dipole moment of an electron (eEDM), the electric counterpart of the magnetic moment, can essentially be caused only by interactions that violate CP symmetry. The CP violation contained within the Standard Model is exceedingly small, well below current experimental sensitivity. In contrast, many extensions to the Standard Model, proposed to help explain the matter-antimatter imbalance, predict eEDMs many orders of magnitude larger and within reach of near-term experiments.

I remember being extremely excited reading about these ideas for the first time as a physics student. In contrast to the enormous infrastructure and huge collaborations involved in running particle colliders like the LHC, experiments to measure everyday particles such as an electron can often fit on a (admittedly large) table in a conventional university laboratory and be handled by a few scientists. It was surprising to me that, in certain cases, these tests can answer questions about fundamental physics that the world's most expensive experiments cannot. The tabletop projects also seemed much better suited to my personality. In large collaborations, individual roles are usually highly specialized; in contrast, running a tabletop experiment requires everyone to take a holistic view of the entire apparatus. We must be generalists, garnering passable knowledge of many different disciplines and technologies, from electronics and computer programming to lasers and vacuum chambers. I love this kind of variety and the chance to do something big with something relatively small.

To say an electron has a nonzero electric dipole moment is equivalent to saying it has a preferred orientation in an electric field—just as the needle of a compass (which has a magnetic dipole moment) has a preferred orientation in Earth's magnetic field. If a compass needle is briefly nudged, it will wobble backward and forward around magnetic north. The frequency of this wobble is proportional to both the strength of the magnetic field and the size of the magnetic dipole moment of the needle.

As a result, if you measure the frequency of the wobble in a known magnetic field, you will know the size of the needle's magnetic dipole moment. If the needle also has an EDM, perhaps because we charged up one end of it somehow, we can measure its size by simultaneously applying an electric field. When the electric field is parallel with the magnetic field, the needle will wobble with a slightly increased frequency; when the electric field is pointing in the opposite direction, the wobble frequency will decrease. The difference between these two frequencies tells us the size of the needle's EDM. We can search for the electron's EDM in precisely the same way, first placing the particle in a magnetic field and then measuring the shift in its wobble frequency when we apply an electric field parallel and then antiparallel to that magnetic field.

We know the eEDM must be very tiny, if it exists at all, so we know we are looking for an extremely tiny shift in the wobble frequency. We can boost the signal by applying a larger electric field. A powerful way to do this is to use electrons confined inside heavy atoms and molecules. You might think that an electron in an atom or molecule wouldn't experience any electric field, or else it would fly away. This is true, however, only if you ignore Einstein's special theory of relativity. When relativity is taken into account, it turns out that in heavy atoms, where relativistic effects are most important because electrons move at close to the speed of light near the highly charged nucleus, the effective electric fields acting on the electron can be tremendous—around a million times larger than the strongest fields we can generate in a lab. To take advantage of this fantastically large field for our measurement, we need apply only enough of an electric field in the lab to orient the atom or molecule. This work turns out to be much easier with molecules, so for the past decade or so all the leading experiments of this type have used electrons in heavy molecules made of two atoms. Our experiment uses hafnium monofluoride molecules because hafnium, with 72 protons in its nucleus, is one of the heaviest metals in the periodic table that isn't radioactive.

Even with this enormous electric field, the change in the wobble frequency of the electron that we might expect from a realistically sized EDM is still very tiny, corresponding to about one extra wobble every seven hours or so. To detect such a minuscule change, we need to measure the two frequencies, with the electric field parallel and then opposite to the direction of the magnetic field, extremely precisely. The longer we monitor a frequency, the more wobbles we can measure and therefore the more precise we can make our measurement.

Our timing is limited by how long our molecules last. For these kinds of experiments, we must use molecules that have free, unpaired electrons, which makes them highly reactive—the electrons are eager to bond with any other atoms they encounter. We have to keep our molecules in vacuum chambers where they don't come into contact with other particles or the walls of the chamber. Previous experiments have used beams of molecules traveling at hundreds of meters per second down a long vacuum chamber, with researchers observing the molecules in free flight. In this setup, the measurement time is limited by how long the beam of molecules can travel before it starts spreading out too much and the signal is lost. Typically this happens within about a meter, or around one millisecond.

For our experiment, we wanted to be able to observe the electrons for longer. We decided to use trapped molecular ions—charged molecules—which we held in position with electric fields. Trapping molecular ions this way isn't new, but no one had previously thought such traps would work for an electric dipole measurement on electrons. These measurements require that we expose our molecules to electric fields, and if the molecules are charged ions, the electric fields should cause them to accelerate away. But the head of our lab, Eric Cornell, had an exciting insight: he suggested that we rotate the electric field fast enough that, instead of flying away, the ions just trace out small circles within the trap. This method let us measure our molecules for three seconds—a great improvement on previous experiments. Our measurement time was limited mainly by the time it took for our molecules to decay into lower-energy states.

Our ion trap technique does have a drawback, though. Because we could trap only so many ions at once, our experiment measured many fewer electrons in each run than typical beam experiments. We were able to observe a few hundred electrons per shot. Over two months of long days in the lab, we measured more than 100 million electrons in total.

Gathering the data set was the quick part. The real challenge of a precision experiment is the time spent looking for systematic errors—ways we might convince ourselves we had measured an eEDM when in fact we had not. Precision-measurement scientists take this job very seriously; no one wants to declare they have discovered new particles only to later find out they had only precisely measured a tiny flaw in their apparatus or method. We spent about two years hunting for and understanding such flaws.

An important source of errors in EDM experiments is the level of control over the magnetic field. Recall that we are looking for a difference in the wobble frequency of an electron in a magnetic field when an electric field is applied parallel to and then opposing the direction of that magnetic field. The problem is that the wobble frequency depends on the strength of the magnetic field. If that field drifts slightly between the two measurements, the result will look like an EDM. To address this possibility, we found a way to do both electric field measurements simultaneously. We take a cloud of molecules and prepare half with their internal electric field aligned with the external magnetic field and half with their internal electric field antialigned. We then measure the wobbles of electrons in both groups simultaneously, and because both are in the same trap at the same time, they experience the same magnetic fields to very high precision.

Another source of systematic error is experimenter bias. All scientists are human beings and, despite our best efforts, can be biased in our thoughts and decisions. This fallibility can potentially affect the results of experiments. In the past it has caused researchers to subconsciously try to match the results of previous experiments. A well-studied example is in measurements of the speed of light. In the late 19th century attempts to determine this constant overestimated it significantly. Later, measurements tended to underestimate the value, leading some physicists to suggest that the speed of light was changing. But in fact, researchers were probably unconsciously steering their data to fit better with previous values, even though those turned out to be inaccurate. It wasn't until experimenters had a much better grasp on the true size of their errors that the various measurements converged on what we now think is the correct value.

To avoid this issue, many modern precision-measurement experiments take data "blinded." In our case, after each run of the experiment, we programmed our computer to add a randomly generated number—the "blind"—to our measurements and store it in an encrypted file. Only after we had gathered all our data, finished our statistical analysis and even mostly written the paper did we have the computer subtract the blind to reveal our true result.

The day of the unveiling was a nerve-racking one. After years of hard work, our team gathered to find out the final result together. I had written a computer program to generate a bingo-style card with 64 plausible numbers, only one of which was the true result. The other numbers varied from "consistent with zero" to "a very significant discovery." Slowly, all the fake answers disappeared from the screen one by one. It's a bit weird to have years of your professional life condensed into a single number, and I questioned the wisdom of amping up the stress with the bingo card. But I think it became apparent to all of us how important the blinding technique was; it was hard to know whether to be relieved or disappointed by the vanishing of a particularly large result that would have hinted at new, undiscovered particles and fields but also contradicted the results of previous experiments.

Finally, a single value remained on the screen. Our answer was consistent with zero within our calculated uncertainty. The result was also consistent with previous measurements, building confidence in them as a collective, and it improved on the best precision by a factor of two. So far, it seems, we have no evidence that the electron has an EDM.

Though perhaps not as exciting as a nonzero value, our new upper limit on the possible size of the eEDM has substantial consequences. If we assume that any new CP-violating field couples to electrons with a strength similar to that of the electromagnetic field (a middling coupling strength in the Standard Model, between those of the fields representing the weak and strong forces), our measurement means that the mass of its associated particle must be more than roughly 40 tera electron volts. This limit would place it far beyond the highest mass of a particle that could be directly discovered at the LHC.

This result, and those of other recent eEDM measurements, is surprising to many who expected new fields to exist below this energy scale. One possible explanation is that the fields couple to the Standard Model in such a way that their contribution to the eEDM is only indirect and therefore smaller for a given mass than the estimate above assumes. Researchers might be able to confirm this possibility by making complementary measurements of EDMs in other particles built from quarks where the coupling is likely to be different. Such measurements are currently underway for neutrons and for mercury nuclei, and many more are planned.

Another possibility is that the new fields are at just slightly higher energies or smaller couplings, out of reach of our experiment but accessible to the next generation of eEDM measurements. I expect the next decade or so to see significant precision improvements. At JILA, we're already working on using a different molecule, thorium fluoride, which has a stronger internal electric field, to increase the observation time still further, perhaps out to 20 seconds. We're also planning to partially address our disadvantage in the number of molecules we can trap by running many copies of the experiment in parallel with tens of separate traps in one long vacuum chamber.

And we expect to see major advances from the latest iteration of the world's best molecular beam experiment, the ACME III project (for "advanced cold molecule EDM"), based at Northwestern University, where scientists are improving the focus of their molecular beam to extend their measurement time. Simultaneously, other physicists are working on ways to trap neutral molecules using laser-cooling techniques. This method could potentially combine the advantages of long measurement times and large numbers of electrons. And an ambitious plan by researchers in Canada aims to study molecules confined inside a solid crystal of frozen noble gas. This technique could enable measurements of colossal numbers of electrons in each shot, but it remains to be seen how the fields from other nearby atoms in the solid will affect the measurement.

Ultimately, we hope to either detect an electric dipole moment in an electron or limit its possible size enough to effectively rule out the types of fields and particles scientists have envisioned to explain our antimatter mystery. We know there must be some reason out there for the universe of matter we live in to be the way it is—the question is how long it will take us to discover it.

About the Author

Luke Caldwell is a lecturer at University College London where his work focuses on using tabletop experiments to test the fundamental laws of physics.

Something Is Wrong with Dark Energy, Physicists Say

By Rebecca Boyle

Imagine sitting in the center of a firework that has just exploded. After the first flash of light and heat, sparks fly off in all directions, with some streaming together into fiery filaments and others fading quickly into cold, ashy oblivion. After a moment more, the smoke is all that remains—the echo, if you will, of the firework's big bang.

Now imagine the firework is the universe, which scientists think began with a similar explosion. Where the firework's expansion is propelled by a chemical reaction, the expansion of the cosmos comes from the energy of empty space itself. From where we sit, it seems that the universe is expanding in all directions, faster and faster at every moment.

This spring scientists announced that something is wrong with the fireworks. For the first time since the discovery of dark energy—the mysterious force that is accelerating our cosmic fireworks show—cosmologists think we may be on the cusp of something new. Two prominent dark energy surveys seeking to measure the nature of this force found evidence that dark energy seems to have weakened over time.

"If it is true, it is a big deal," says Licia Verde, a theoretical cosmologist at the Institute of Cosmos Sciences of the University of Barcelona in Spain and a member of the collaboration reporting the oddity. "But as usual, extraordinary claims require extraordinary proofs."

Dark energy was assumed to be a constant force in the universe, as unchanging and reliable as the forward march of time. If the new results are right, it is changeable after all. "It's mega important," says Paul J. Steinhardt, a cosmologist at Princeton University, who did not work on the data, adding that this is only true if the results hold up to scrutiny. "But it's still early days."

The news is based on a combination of two dark energy studies, called the Dark Energy Survey (DES) and the Dark Energy Spectroscopic Instrument (DESI), with a third set of preexisting data. DES measures distant supernovae, and the DESI experiment measures galaxies and sound waves from the early universe. The third component measures the cosmic microwave background (CMB)—the smoke ring of the cosmic firework.

DES yielded new findings back in February, and DESI came out with novel results in April. The DESI data produced a detailed three-dimensional map of the universe. It showed that galaxies appear to be spread apart less than they should be if dark energy's role was unchanging through cosmic time.

The DESI telescope is perched on Kitt Peak in Arizona and measures the positions of millions of galaxies as they existed between 12 billion and two billion years ago. Astronomers compared these observed galactic locales against where galaxies are expected to be based on dark energy predictions and saw the lack of expected spreading.

A bigger surprise came when cosmologists combined the DESI galaxies, DES's supernovae and the cosmic microwave background. The map of reality began to drift apart from theory.

Theorists have been buzzing since: if the results are true, a bedrock assumption of cosmology is incorrect. Scientists might have to throw out the widely held idea that dark energy is a "cosmological constant"—a static element of the universe.

"If the cosmological constant is wrong, all bets are off about what's right," says Adam G. Riess, a cosmologist at Johns Hopkins University, who shared the 2011 Nobel Prize in Physics for the discovery of dark energy and did not work on the new results.

To understand what's wrong, we have to go back to Albert Einstein. When he was formulating his general theory of relativity, he assumed that the universe was evenly spread out and stationary. This idea was bold in 1917, when we didn't even know there were other galaxies and the evidence suggested that stars were not spread out evenly. But in Einstein's equations, gravity and uniformity don't get along. Gravity causes instability. If gravity was dominant in a curved universe, then everything in the cosmos should clump together into one big blob—but it doesn't. Einstein assumed there must be some cosmic force counteracting gravity, which he called a "cosmological constant" and described using the Greek letter Lambda. In 1929, however, Edwin Hubble showed that the universe was not static but expanding, so Einstein abandoned this constant counteracting force, calling it his "biggest blunder."

In 1998 Riess, as well as cosmologists Saul Perlmutter of the University of California, Berkeley and Brian P. Schmidt of the Australian National University showed that Einstein was right the first time. The researchers saw that supernovae that exploded when the universe was young were fainter than would be expected, which implied the universe was expanding outward ever faster, presumably because of an omnipresent and unchanging force. The cosmological constant was resurrected. Scientists believe that the force behind the constant must come from energy present in empty space, which they call vacuum energy, or dark energy. In this view, as the universe expands, each new bit of the growing vacuum comes with its own vacuum energy, so the total amount of dark energy grows, causing the cosmic expansion to continue to accelerate. (Dark energy is still a constant because, although its total rises as the universe grows, the amount of energy in each piece of space—the energy density—is constant.) What's more, the constant value of dark energy was set at the big bang and then never lessened. Bang, zap: the universe has the same inherent energy everywhere, all at once.

All observations since the late 1990s have seemed to confirm this scenario. Lambda is now the heart of the standard model of cosmology, which combines dark energy with the gravitation of copious, invisible "cold dark matter" (CDM), known as Lambda-CDM. This standard model holds that about 68 percent of the universe is made up of dark energy, another 27 percent is dark matter, and the remaining 5 percent is everything we can see and measure: galaxies, stars, whales, us. Surveys like DESI were designed to measure dark energy precisely enough to understand its quirks.

Still, not everyone has been satisfied with the Lambda-CDM model. "It seems like a very peculiar set of affairs," Steinhardt says. "The only thing that's nice about it is that it is described by a single number. But that doesn't mean you should believe it. And if it turns out that dark energy is time-varying, that opens up a lot of possibilities."

Theorists have been increasingly busy since the DESI results and the combined 3D map both dropped in April. So far, no single theory can supplant Lambda with some other nonconstant cosmological force. Even before the new results, some cosmologists favored alternatives to a constant dark energy, in part because the idea is so weird—other known forces are not constant but vary with time, pressure and other factors—and in part because Lambda is nonsensical when inserted into other physics theories. "In quantum theory, if you calculate the energy of empty space, you don't get a sensible answer. You get infinity," says Joshua A. Frieman, a cosmologist at the University of Chicago, who co-founded DES to study this problem and is not involved in the new DESI results. "That's one reason people have looked for alternatives: we don't understand why it would have this value."

Theorists have several ideas for new kinds of dark energy, most of which involve a fluidlike energy field, reminiscent of the Higgs field that endows normal particles with mass. The proposed dark energy field is often called "quintessence," after a classic fifth element first imagined in antiquity. There are a few ways such an energy field, also called a scalar field, could work. It would produce the same results we can see—galaxies flung apart from one another and an apparently expanding empty canvas on which to see them—but the difference is that the cosmological force is temporary, not everlasting and unchanging.

Some theorists favor quintessence because they already study a potential earlier version of a scalar field called cosmic inflation. This field would have affected the universe immediately after the big bang, driving it to expand exponentially before eventually calming down and continuing to accelerate at a slower rate. A scalar field underlying modern dark energy is like "inflation lite," according to Riess. Where there is energy in the physical space of the universe, the universe will accelerate. The dark energy field would be exceptionally weak, about 30 orders of magnitude lighter than the Higgs field. And it would be temporary like inflation was.

One popular version, first proposed by Frieman and his collaborators in 1995, is called "thawing" or "slowly rolling" dark energy. Its effects on the universe would be similar to those of a cosmological constant—to a point, says Jessie Muir, a theoretical cosmologist at the Perimeter Institute. "It acts like empty space has some intrinsic energy density," she says, "but because it changes in the later universe, you can get some deviations at later times."

Think of a ball rolling down one side of a hill toward a shallow, U-shaped valley. If there is no friction, the ball will roll up the opposite side, then roll back down and oscillate back and forth. The ball represents the field's potential, which describes how easy it is to move that field in relation to the density or expansion of the universe, Muir says. This is also one way to understand the Higgs field, which physicists think underwent some changes early in the universe before it reached its current state. A similar but much heavier field could have driven cosmic inflation. If dark energy works in the same way, there's precedent for it, Frieman says.

"In the only other case of acceleration we know about [inflation], we know it wasn't dark energy, the constant. It was something else," he says. "I've always felt we need to keep an open mind about what is driving the current accelerated expansion of the universe." In Frieman's versions of this theory, you put the ball on one side of the hill at the beginning of the universe. The ball is stuck at first because the universe is too dense for it to roll quickly. As the universe expands and matter dilutes, the ball can begin to roll. This is called a "thawing" dark energy model because the ball unfreezes and begins to move. "That is acting like dark energy but dark energy that has a different impact on the expansion of the universe than if it was exactly constant," Frieman says. "And it can look exactly like what the recent results from DESI and the Dark Energy Survey and CMB data seem to be suggesting."

Theorists are also testing ideas such as the "big bounce," a cyclic universe in which the big bang happens again and again, as well as variations on general relativity in which gravity behaves differently in the very early universe or on different scales, among other possibilities.

A flurry of scientific papers are being uploaded to the preprint server arXiv.org, where cosmologists are sharing ideas and paths forward. Everything is on the table, from arguments about the masses of particles called neutrinos to discussions of the best statistical methods for comparing data. "I wouldn't say there is a specific model so far that seems to be taking the lead," says Nathalie Palanque-Delabrouille, a cosmologist at Lawrence Berkeley National Laboratory and a spokesperson for the DESI project. "There are too many hypotheses out there, and many models can fit the data. That's why it's important to keep going."

A coming generation of new observatories will shed light on dark energy—or whatever other force is driving the expansion of the universe. The Euclid space telescope, operated by the European Space Agency, launched last year and will work until 2030 to create a map of almost one third of the sky, charting dark matter and dark energy. NASA's future Nancy Grace Roman Space Telescope will measure more than a billion galaxies to study dark energy over time. And the DESI survey will continue through 2026.

For Lambda to fall, cosmologists would want a five-sigma level of confidence, which means about a one-in-a-million chance that the findings are a result of error or random chance. So far, the DESI, DES and cosmic microwave background results from the Planck satellite show a probability of three sigma, which is about a 0.3 percent probability of something happening by chance. While this sounds like strong evidence, three-sigma results can fail under scrutiny, so a five-sigma finding is necessary for a real discovery. DESI is continuing its work, but the team already has another year of galactic data to examine, and Verde says her colleagues are clamoring for it. "I am working until my hands are on fire," she says.

Muir, who also studies general relativity and tests of gravity at different scales, says the universe as it is will provide the best clues. If dark energy is a fluidlike energy field like quintessence, then models would predict a certain type of relationship between how the universe has expanded over time and how cosmic structures have come together. Cosmologists can look for correlations between expansion and growth, such as the formation of galaxy clusters, to understand both quintessence and gravity beyond general relativity, she says.

Even Verde, who is working on the DESI analysis, remains skeptical that Lambda-CDM will be overturned. "I am really conservative, but on whether I am willing personally to throw constant dark energy out the window based on this—not yet," she says. "Right now we need to keep looking at it and understand it better."

Many cosmologists are paying close attention but not eulogizing Lambda quite yet, Riess says. Steinhardt suggests systematic errors could play a role in the new findings, especially when three different types of data are combined to arrive at one sweeping conclusion. "Everyone is doing the best they can, but you should take it with a large grain of salt," he says.

If Lambda lives, in some ways, that will be a very boring outcome—and a philosophically challenging one. The future of the universe will be cold, empty, distant and quiet. Expansion will accelerate forever until atoms themselves are stretched so thin that their centers will not hold, and they fall apart.

But maybe the future is brighter than that, Frieman says. "These hints from DESI and DES are telling us to keep going," he adds.

About the Author

Rebecca Boyle is a Scientific American *contributor and an award-winning freelance journalist in Colorado. Her new book,* Our Moon: How Earth's Celestial Companion Transformed the Planet, Guided Evolution, and Made Us Who We Are *(Random House), explores Earth's relation with its satellite.*

Section 3: Health and the Mind

3.1 Schizophrenia's Unyielding Mysteries
By Michael Balter

3.2 What's So Funny? The Science of Why We Laugh
By Giovanni Sabato

3.3 How Old Can Humans Get?
By Bill Gifford

Schizophrenia's Unyielding Mysteries
By Michael Balter

Last year, when researchers in Cambridge, Mass., announced that they had found a gene strongly linked to a higher risk of schizophrenia, the news media reacted with over-zealous enthusiasm. A "landmark study," declared both the *New York Times* and the *Washington Post*. "Ground-breaking," trumpeted CNN. Even the *Economist* dropped its normal reserve: "Genetics throws open a window on a perplexing disorder."

The hype was somewhat understandable. Historically, schizophrenia research has left a trail of disappointment. The biological basis of the illness, one of the most puzzling and complex mental disorders, has long been an enigma. The toll, however, has always been clear. In the U.S. alone, estimates place the total cost of caring for patients at more than $60 billion a year, a figure that includes both direct health care costs and indirect economic losses from unemployment and early death. Any breakthrough in understanding the causes of the illness would be a major medical advance.

Since the advent of large-scale genetic studies just more than a decade ago, hopes have risen that new insights and therapies were on the way. They are much needed. Existing antipsychotic drugs dampen only the most overt symptoms, such as delusions and hallucinations. They often cause serious side effects and do little or nothing for chronic symptoms such as social withdrawal and cognitive deficits.

But genetic studies have yet to deliver on this promise. Gargantuan gene studies for schizophrenia, as well as depression and obsessive-compulsive and bipolar disorders, have driven home the message that most likely no single gene will lead to new treatments. The study behind last year's exuberant headlines was no exception. If nothing else, though, that research provides an inside look at the immense difficulties in understanding the mental processes that veer off course in schizophrenia.

The 1 Percent

Scientists who study psychiatric disorders had solid reasons to think that genetic clues might help overcome the field's stagnation. Decades of family and twin research suggest a strong genetic component to schizophrenia risk—one underlined by the steady rate at which the disorder occurs. Its prevalence is estimated to be about 1 percent throughout the world, notwithstanding vast environmental and socioeconomic differences across societies. Geneticists also knew that the hunt would not be straightforward. Individual genes powerful enough to generate a high risk of schizophrenia were likely to be very rare in the overall population and thus relevant to only a small percentage of schizophrenia cases. More common genes, on the other hand, would have much smaller effects in triggering schizophrenia and thus be much harder to detect. To find them would require greater statistical power, which would mean working with big sample sizes—tens of thousands of cases and control subjects. Acknowledging the challenges at hand, scientists in 2007 launched the Psychiatric Genomics Consortium (PGC) to study schizophrenia and other mental disorders. At present, the PGC has more than 800 collaborators from 38 countries and samples from more than 900,000 subjects.

Michael O'Donovan, a psychiatric geneticist at Cardiff University in Wales and chair of the PGC's schizophrenia working group, says a global approach was essential to assembling the "truly enormous sample sizes" needed to do the job in what is known as a genome-wide association study (GWAS). A big splash came in July 2014, when the group reported a GWAS involving about 37,000 schizophrenia cases and 113,000 control subjects. The study identified 108 genes (genetic regions) linked to schizophrenia, including a number that code for brain-signaling systems, the main targets for current antipsychotic drugs. These correlations were a sign that researchers might be on the right track.

The genetic region that showed the strongest link to schizophrenia codes for proteins of the major histocompatibility complex (MHC), which is intimately involved in recognizing molecules alien to the body and alerting the immune system. That discovery led Steven McCarroll, a geneticist at the Broad Institute of Harvard University and the Massachusetts Institute of Technology, to think that the MHC region might be a good target for additional study. When McCarroll's team probed further, it turned up a variant of *C4*, an MHC gene, that elevated schizophrenia risk from about 1 to 1.27 percent in the populations studied.

Although that is a relatively small increase, the researchers suggested in their report in *Nature* that it could hint at how some cases of schizophrenia arise. The *C4* results were important for other reasons as well. Variations in human *C4* consist not only of differences in the gene's DNA sequence but also of disparities in its length and how many copies of that gene an individual has.

From previous studies, scientists suspected that relatively rare copy number variations (CNVs) played important roles in schizophrenia—and they continue to debate whether key schizophrenia genes are likely to be uncommon variants that raise risk dramatically or common versions that increase risk only slightly. The new study provided strong confirmation of CNVs' tie to schizophrenia. And when the team compared the brains of both living and deceased schizophrenia patients with those of control subjects, it found that markedly more of the C4 protein was produced in the patients' brains, which was associated with the presence of additional copies of the gene.

To look more closely at what *C4* does at the molecular level, the researchers turned to mouse brains. Beth Stevens of the Broad Institute, who spearheaded this part of the study, found that the protein assisted in brain development by "pruning" neural connections, called synapses, when they are no longer needed. Synaptic pruning is a normal part of brain maturation. But if this process is overactive and pares back too many synapses, it could perhaps elucidate some of the features of schizophrenia. It might explain why affected patients tend to have thinner cerebral cortexes and fewer synapses. And schizophrenia, along with other forms of psychosis, is usually first diagnosed in people in their late teens or early adulthood, when brain maturation reaches its final stages.

For some scientists, the finding was a vindication for GWAS as a relatively new way to hunt down disease-associated genes. GWAS has triggered an "amazingly positive and unprecedented explosion of new knowledge" about mental disorders, says Patrick Sullivan, a psychiatric geneticist at the University of North Carolina at Chapel Hill School of Medicine. As for the *C4* study, David Goldstein, director of Columbia University's Institute for Genomic Medicine—who has long been a skeptic of GWAS's potential—says that by pointing the way to a possible biological pathway for schizophrenia, the new finding represents "the first time we have gotten what we wanted out of a GWAS." Others, including some leading geneticists, are less certain, however. "GWAS will have no impact on resolving the biology of schizophrenia," says Mary-Claire King of the University of Washington, who in 1990 identified *BRCA1* as a major risk gene for breast cancer.

In scientific parlance, most cases of schizophrenia appear to be highly "polygenic"—hundreds or perhaps thousands of genes are involved. "GWAS shows that schizophrenia is so highly, radically polygenic that there may well be nothing to find, just a general unspecifiable genetic background," says Eric Turkheimer, a behavioral geneticist at the University of Virginia.

Indeed, it might be argued that one of GWAS's most important contributions—and the *C4* study was no exception—has been to disabuse researchers of simplistic notions about psychiatric genetics. The new findings so far have dashed hopes that schizophrenia can be pinned on just one or even a few genetic mutations. The skepticism stems from the realization that each of the 108 genetic locations linked to schizophrenia so far confers only a tiny risk for the disorder. And the few genes that confer a high risk—in the case of copy number variants and other rare mutations—account for only a small percentage of schizophrenia cases. That makes it less likely that the new findings will lead to therapies anytime soon. It also poses obstacles for neuroscientists and psychiatrists who hoped to find genetic clues for the underlying roots of the disorder. "It would have been way better if there were one single gene," says Kenneth Kendler, a psychiatric researcher at the Virginia Commonwealth University's School of Medicine. "Then all of our research could have gone into that area."

In the case of *C4*, a recognition of these limitations has led to questions about just how relevant the gene will be to understanding schizophrenia or developing new therapies. Whereas about 27 percent of the nearly 29,000 schizophrenia patients in the study had the highest-risk *C4* variant, roughly 22 percent of the 36,000 healthy control subjects also carry it, according to McCarroll. "Even if the *C4* story is right, it accounts for only a trivial amount of schizophrenia," says Kenneth Weiss, an evolutionary geneticist at Pennsylvania State University. "How useful that will be is debatable." And the study does not prove a direct relation between synaptic pruning and schizophrenia, McCarroll and others concede. Its importance seems to lie more in its potential to help pinpoint what kinds of biological pathways might be involved.

Still other problems beset GWAS. To procure huge samples, geneticists usually distinguish between cases and controls depending on whether a person has received a formal schizophrenia diagnosis or not. But the criteria are very broad. In the U.S., the diagnostic rules are dictated by the American Psychiatric Association's *Diagnostic and Statistical Manual of Mental Disorders*, whereas many psychiatrists in other countries rely on the World Health Organization's International *Classification of Diseases*. In the criteria set out in both volumes, patients can have markedly different symptoms, ranging from delusions to hallucinations to cognitive defects, and still be diagnosed with a case of schizophrenia.

Hannelore Ehrenreich, a neuroscientist at the Max Planck Institute of Experimental Medicine in Göttingen, Germany, describes schizophrenia as "an umbrella diagnosis" rather than a distinct disease: "We are focusing on people who are on the extreme end of human experience, who are part of a continuum and not a separate category." William Carpenter, a psychiatrist at the University of Maryland School of Medicine and editor in chief of the flagship journal *Schizophrenia Bulletin*, does not go that far, but he acknowledges that schizophrenia is a group of disorders or symptoms and not a distinct disease. "That makes it a weak target for gene discovery," he says.

Goldstein, who thinks the *C4* findings "are the best case we've got" for understanding how a schizophrenia risk gene might exert its effects, still calls for researchers to express "a whole lot more humility" about GWAS results. "People working in the schizophrenia genetics field have greatly overinterpreted their results."

Some of the strongest skepticism about the search for schizophrenia genes comes from psychiatrists, patient advocates and former patients themselves. The GWAS approach focuses on finding new drugs to lessen symptoms of the disorder. But patients often look askance at this goal. "This obsession with symptom reduction does not entirely correspond with the viewpoint of the patients," says Jim van Os, a psychiatrist at the Maastricht University Medical Center in the Netherlands. Rather, van Os says, patients want to be able to live productive lives and function in society—and doing so does not necessarily correspond with being more medicated.

Van Os and a growing number of patient advocates argue that the term "schizophrenia" itself is part of the problem because it stigmatizes and dehumanizes patients without adequately describing what is wrong with them. Jim Geekie, a clinical psychologist who works at a National Health Service inpatient unit just outside London, says that "knowing somebody's diagnosis tells me next to nothing about them."

Indeed, a number of countries and regions in Asia, including Japan, South Korea, Hong Kong and Singapore, have eliminated the classification altogether. The Japanese term "mind-split disease," used to describe a person with schizophrenia, has been changed to "integration disorder," and a similar term in Korean has been changed to "attunement disorder."

For many researchers and advocates, the main problem with the nomenclature—and with the gene search itself—is the lingering implication that patients are suffering from a form of brain disease. "If there are genetic variations that mean some people are prone to having these experiences, then we need to make sure people's environments don't switch these things on," says Jacqui Dillon, chair of the U.K.'s Hearing Voices Network. Dillon, who was told as a young woman that she had schizophrenia and still hears voices today, adds that understanding schizophrenia genetics "doesn't change what we need to do to keep people from going mad."

A Deep Flaw

Some researchers insist that the search for genes is misguided because it largely ignores the environmental context, as well as the personal and family circumstances, that contributes to schizophrenia risk. "The whole enterprise is deeply flawed," says University of Liverpool psychologist Richard Bentall. This view is especially strong among clinicians, such as Bentall, who directly treat schizophrenia patients. They argue for increased funding for pragmatic, nonbiological approaches, ranging from family therapy to cognitive-behavioral therapy (CBT).

At times, questions also arise about the fundamental idea, derived largely from family and twin studies, that schizophrenia has a high "heritability." This term is often assumed, even by many scientists, to mean that genetic factors play a major role. Yet the concept of heritability is complex and not a direct measure of how "genetic" a particular trait—such as a formal schizophrenia diagnosis—actually is [see *"Heritability: Missing or Just Hiding?"* on pages 80–82].

In fact, environmental and social factors, some researchers insist, confer a greater schizophrenia risk than most genes identified so far. Epidemiological studies have shown that risk factors range from living in an urban environment or being an immigrant to experiencing poverty and emotional and sexual abuse.

Just how such factors contribute to schizophrenia risk is not well understood, aside from speculations that they are sources of emotional stress. Recently, for example, an Israeli team found that Holocaust survivors suffered higher rates of schizophrenia. Another group found increased risk among people who had lived through the violent "Troubles" in Northern Ireland.

There is growing evidence that progress can be made only if researchers consider a spectrum of risk factors. Whereas genetics may make some people more vulnerable to mental disorders, influences from family or a social circle may push a susceptible individual across a threshold that results in a first psychotic episode. The key task is to figure out how genetic and environmental factors interact to produce schizophrenia.

Even diehard gene jockeys admit that environmental influences must be playing some kind of role. "Genes are not destiny," McCarroll agrees. He points out that when one member of a pair of identical twins is diagnosed with schizophrenia, the other twin is affected by the disorder only about half of the time—a clear indication that nongenetic factors must be important.

Environmental Roots

Frustrations in the hunt for schizophrenia genes have forced the field to reassess how to move forward. Genetics is still considered important to understanding the biological underpinnings of the disorder and coming up with new drugs. But most researchers and clinicians now agree that a broader strategy that supplements genomic approaches is needed, one that builds on expertise gained from experts in sociology, psychotherapy and even prenatal health.

Over the past several years psychologists, psychiatrists, epidemiologists and social workers have accumulated a deeper understanding of the environmental and social factors underlying the disorder. Many new studies are now focusing on "childhood adversity," an umbrella term that includes sexual, physical and emotional abuse, neglect, bullying, and the loss of one or more parents.

One of the most widely cited of these studies, a meta-analysis by van Os and his colleagues, published in 2012 in *Schizophrenia Bulletin*, combined results from several studies to increase statistical power and found that patients suffering psychotic symptoms were nearly three times as likely to have been the victims of adversity, far greater than the risk of any gene identified so far in a GWAS. "We need a stronger focus on changing the environment so we can prevent schizophrenia," says Roar Fosse, a neuroscientist at the Vestre Viken Hospital Trust in Norway. "We need to give children better childhoods and better chances to avoid extreme stress."

And in a 2014 paper in the *Lancet*, Ehrenreich and her colleagues demonstrated how studies that combine genetic and environmental data can provide new insights. The team reported on 750 male schizophrenia patients in Germany for whom—unusually—both GWAS and detailed environmental and social risk data were available. The team looked at the age of schizophrenia onset in these patients, a key indicator of how well they are likely to do over the long run: the earlier the age of onset, the worse the eventual outcome. It found that environmental factors, including early brain damage, childhood trauma, living in an urban environment, coming from an immigrant family, and especially cannabis use, were significantly associated with earlier onset. The average age of onset was nearly 10 years earlier for patients who had four or more environmental risk factors than for those who had none. On the other hand, so-called polygenic risk scores calculated from the GWAS data had no detectable effect on age of onset.

Ehrenreich does not interpret these results to mean that genes are irrelevant. It is more likely, she says, that "the genetic factors are so different from one individual to the next that each person has a different reason for having the disorder." Other researchers, meanwhile, are looking at how environmental stresses, at home or school or through exposure to certain chemicals, might turn genes off and on—a pursuit known as epigenetics.

Ehrenreich and others urge GWAS researchers to begin incorporating environmental data into their studies whenever possible so they can derive a statistical model of how genes and environment interact to make people sick. "It is a shame that researchers neglect assessing environmental information in some of the most expensive and technologically advanced genetic studies," says Rudolf Uher, a psychiatric researcher at Dalhousie University in Nova Scotia.

Unfortunately, combining epidemiology with genetics may be a tall order. "The cost of gathering environmental data is enormous, and there is considerable disagreement about how to define these environmental variables," Cardiff's O'Donovan comments. Even so, in 2010 the European Union funded a five-year pilot program to do just that, led by O'Donovan, van Os and others—and researchers have now begun analyzing the data generated.

The big question, of course, is whether the search for genes, even in the context of environmental influences, will eventually lead to new therapies. Most scientists agree that it will take many more years for this research to pay off in new drugs or other interventions. Genetics "has provided the first hard biological leads in understanding schizophrenia," says Peter Visscher, a geneticist at the University of Queensland in Brisbane, Australia. "It is too early to say whether these discoveries will lead to new therapies, but there is no reason why they could not." Psychiatric researcher John McGrath, also at Queensland, agrees: "The science is hard, and the brain is hard to understand. But there is no need to throw our hands up in despair."

Meanwhile, in parallel with the genetic studies, schizophrenia researchers are pursuing numerous other lines of inquiry. They have begun looking for biomarkers—telltale molecules in blood or brain anomalies from neuroimaging that might help them identify people at high risk for the disorder. This could lead to earlier treatment, which numerous studies demonstrate can lead to a better long-term prognosis. Prompted by studies suggesting that the children of women who come down with infectious diseases during pregnancy might be at higher risk for schizophrenia—possibly because of immune responses harmful to the brain of the fetus—other teams are testing anti-inflammatory compounds to see if they might reduce symptoms.

A number of recent clinical trials, meanwhile, suggest that psychosocial therapies, especially CBT, can help lessen both symptoms and suffering in schizophrenia patients. While this research is controversial and the effects are only modest so far, advocates of such approaches are gaining traction in both Europe and the U.S. In the U.K., for example, CBT is now recommended by government health authorities for all first-episode cases of psychosis. "The imbalance in funding between genetic and pharmacological research and psychosocial research needs to be addressed and corrected," says Brian Koehler, a neuroscientist at New York University who also treats schizophrenia patients in private practice.

The intricacies of schizophrenia mean that comprehensive new treatments are still speculative. Researchers hope that one day brain imaging or other diagnostic tests may help spot a youngster at risk either before or during adolescence. If so, new medications and psychological counseling may be able to delay or prevent a first psychotic break. To achieve that goal, biologists and social scientists must continue to merge their expertise to piece together a composite profile of one of the most complex of all psychiatric illnesses.

Heritability: Missing or Just Hiding?

Researchers have been looking for schizophrenia-related genes for at least 50 years. What makes them think they will find them? The rationale is spelled out in the introduction to nearly every scientific paper on schizophrenia genetics: The disorder has a high heritability. This term is often interpreted as a measure of the relative role played by genes. Heritability is usually expressed as a percentage between 0 and 100 percent.

Scientists have estimated the heritability of schizophrenia using several approaches, including studies of twins. Most estimates hover around 80 percent. Many researchers argue that heritability estimates for schizophrenia can be very misleading, however. They question key suppositions, including the so-called equal environment assumption (EEA), which considers both identical and fraternal twins to be subject to the same environmental influences.

"These basic assumptions are wrong," says Roar Fosse, a neuroscientist at the Vestre Viken Hospital Trust in Norway, who led a recent critical assessment of the EEA. But twin researchers have mounted a vigorous defense of the approach. "I don't think it's likely that current heritability numbers are substantially overestimated," says Kenneth Kendler, a psychiatrist at the Virginia Commonwealth University's School of Medicine.

Some researchers have an even more profound critique of heritability. They argue that the technical calculations of the term do not account for the relative role of genes and environment. Heritability, rather, measures only how much the variation of a trait in a particular population—whether height, IQ or being diagnosed with schizophrenia—reflects genetic differences in that group.

As an example of how misleading heritability estimates can be, Eric Turkheimer, a geneticist at the University of Virginia, points to the human trait of having two arms. Nearly everyone in a given population has two of them, and there is normally no difference in the number of arms between identical twins—who share nearly 100 percent of their DNA sequence—and fraternal twins, who are assumed to share 50 percent of their genes on average. Thus, when heritability for arm number is calculated using standard heritability equations, it comes out to 0. And yet we know that having two arms is almost entirely genetically determined.

Figuring out what heritability for schizophrenia actually means is key, researchers say, because even the most high-powered genetic studies have identified only about a third of the predicted genetic component. Will this so-called missing heritability eventually show up in more sophisticated studies—

or will it turn out that genes are not playing as big a role as heritability estimates have long predicted? The jury is still out.

—M.B.

Referenced

"The Environment and Schizophrenia." Jim van Os et al. in *Nature*, Vol. 468, pages 203–212; November 11, 2010.

"Rethinking Schizophrenia." Thomas R. Insel in *Nature*, Vol. 468, pages 187–193; November 11, 2010.

"Talking Back to Madness." Michael Balter in *Science*, Vol. 343, pages 1190–1193; March 14, 2014.

"Schizophrenia." René S. Kahn et al. in *Nature Reviews Disease Primers*, Vol. 1, Article No. 15067; 2015.

"Schizophrenia Risk from Complex Variation of Complement Component 4." Aswin Sekar et al. in *Nature*, Vol. 530, pages 177–183; February 11, 2016.

About the Author

Michael Balter is a freelance journalist, whose articles have appeared in Audubon, National Geographic *and* Science, *among other publications.*

What's So Funny? The Science of Why We Laugh

By Giovanni Sabato

"How Many Psychologists Does It Take ... to Explain a Joke?"

Many, it turns out. As psychologist Christian Jarrett noted in a 2013 article featuring that riddle as its title, scientists still struggle to explain exactly what makes people laugh. Indeed, the concept of humor is itself elusive. Although everyone understands intuitively what humor is, and dictionaries may define it simply as "the quality of being amusing," it is difficult to define in a way that encompasses all its aspects. It may evoke the merest smile or explosive laughter; it can be conveyed by words, images or actions and through photos, films, skits or plays; and it can take a wide range of forms, from innocent jokes to biting sarcasm and from physical gags and slapstick to a cerebral double entendre.

Even so, progress has been made. And some of the research has come out of the lab to investigate humor in its natural habitat: everyday life.

Superiority and Relief

For more than 2,000 years pundits have assumed that all forms of humor share a common ingredient. The search for this essence occupied first philosophers and then psychologists, who formalized the philosophical ideas and translated them into concepts that could be tested.

Perhaps the oldest theory of humor, which dates back to Plato and other ancient Greek philosophers, posits that people find humor in, and laugh at, earlier versions of themselves and the misfortunes of others because of feeling superior.

The 18th century gave rise to the theory of release. The best-known version, formulated later by Sigmund Freud, held that laughter allows people to let off steam or release pent-up "nervous energy." According to Freud, this process explains why tabooed scatological and sexual themes and jokes that broach thorny social and ethnic topics can amuse us. When the punch line comes, the energy being expended to suppress inappropriate emotions, such as desire or hostility, is no longer needed and is released as laughter.

A third long-standing explanation of humor is the theory of incongruity. People laugh at the juxtaposition of incompatible concepts and at defiance of their expectations—that is, at the incongruity between expectations and reality. According to a variant of the theory known as resolution of incongruity, laughter results when a person discovers an unexpected solution to an apparent incongruity, such as when an individual grasps a double meaning in a statement and thus sees the statement in a completely new light.

Benign Violation

These and other explanations all capture something, and yet they are insufficient. They do not provide a complete theoretical framework with a hypothesis that can be measured using well-defined parameters. They also do not explain all types of humor. None, for example, seems to fully clarify the appeal of slapstick. In 2010 in the journal *Psychological Science*, A. Peter McGraw and Caleb Warren, both then at the University of Colorado Boulder, proposed a theory they call "benign violation" to unify the previous theories and to address their limits. "It's a very interesting idea," says Delia Chiaro, a linguist at the University of Bologna in Italy.

McGraw and Warren's hypothesis derives from the theory of incongruity, but it goes deeper. Humor results, they propose, when a person simultaneously recognizes both that an ethical, social or physical norm has been violated and that this violation is not very offensive, reprehensible or upsetting. Hence, someone who judges a violation as no big deal will be amused, whereas someone who finds it scandalous, disgusting or simply uninteresting will not.

Experimental findings from studies conducted by McGraw and Warren corroborate the hypothesis. Consider, for example, the story of a church that recruits the faithful by entering into a raffle for an SUV anyone who joins in the next six months. Study participants all judged the situation to be incongruous, but only nonbelievers readily laughed at it.

Levity can also partly be a product of distance from a situation— for example, in time. It has been said that humor is tragedy plus time, and McGraw, Warren and their colleagues lent support to that notion in 2012, once again in *Psychological Science*. The recollection of serious misfortunes (a car accident, for example, that had no lasting effects to keep its memory fresh) can seem more amusing the more time passes.

Geographical or emotional remoteness lends a bit of distance as well, as does viewing a situation as imaginary. In another test, volunteers were amused by macabre photos (such as a man with a finger stuck up his nose and out his eye) if the images were presented as effects created with Photoshop, but participants were less amused if told the images were authentic. Conversely, people laughed more at banal anomalies (a man with a frozen beard) if they believed them to be true. McGraw argues that there seems to be an optimal comic point where the balance is just right between how bad a thing is and how distant it is.

Evolutionary Theory

The idea of benign violation has limitations, however: it describes triggers of laughter but does not explain, for instance, the role humor has played in humanity's evolutionary success. Several other theories, all of which contain elements of older concepts, try to explain humor from an evolutionary vantage. Gil Greengross, an anthropologist then at the University of New Mexico, noted that humor and laughter occur in every society, as well as in apes and even rats. This universality suggests an evolutionary role, although humor and laughter could conceivably be a byproduct of some other process important to survival.

In a 2005 issue of the *Quarterly Review of Biology*, evolutionary biologist David Sloan Wilson and his colleague Matthew Gervais, both then at Binghamton University, S.U.N.Y., offered an explanation of the evolutionary benefits of humor. Wilson is a major proponent of group selection, an evolutionary theory based on the idea that in social species like ours, natural selection favors characteristics that foster the survival of the group, not just of individuals

Wilson and Gervais applied the concept of group selection to two different types of human laughter. Spontaneous, emotional, impulsive and involuntary laughter is a genuine expression of amusement and joy and is a reaction to playing and joking around; it shows up in the smiles of a child or during roughhousing or tickling. This display of amusement is called Duchenne laughter, after scholar Guillaume-Benjamin-Amand Duchenne de Boulogne, who first described it in the mid-19th century. Conversely, non-Duchenne laughter is a studied and not very emotional imitation of spontaneous laughter. People employ it as a voluntary social strategy—for example, when their smiles and laughter punctuate ordinary conversations, even when those chats are not particularly funny.

Facial expressions and the neural pathways that control them differ between the two kinds of laughter, the authors say. Duchenne laughter arises in the brain stem and the limbic system (responsible for emotions), whereas non-Duchenne laughter is controlled by the voluntary premotor areas (thought to participate in planning movements) of the frontal cortex. The neural mechanisms are so distinct that just one pathway or the other is affected in some forms of facial paralysis. According to Wilson and Gervais, the two forms of laughter, and the neural mechanisms behind them, evolved at different times. Spontaneous laughter has its roots in the games of early primates and in fact has features in common with animal vocalizations. Controlled laughter may have evolved later, with the development of casual conversation, denigration and derision in social interactions.

Ultimately, the authors suggest, primate laughter was gradually co-opted and elaborated through human biological and cultural evolution in several stages. Between four and two million years ago Duchenne laughter became a medium of emotional contagion, a social glue, in long-extinct human ancestors; it promoted interactions among members of a group in periods of safety and satiation. Laughter by group members in response to what Wilson and Gervais call protohumor—nonserious violations of social norms—was a reliable indicator of such relaxed, safe times and paved the way to playful emotions.

When later ancestors acquired more sophisticated cognitive and social skills, Duchenne laughter and protohumor became the basis for humor in all its most complex facets and for new functions. Now non-Duchenne laughter, along with its dark side, appeared: strategic, calculated, and even derisory and aggressive.

Over the years additional theories have proposed different explanations for humor's role in evolution, suggesting that humor and laughter could play a part in the selection of sexual partners and the damping of aggression and conflict.

Spot the Mistake

One of the more recent proposals appears in a 2011 book dedicated to an evolutionary explanation of humor, *Inside Jokes: Using Humor to Reverse-Engineer the Mind* (MIT Press, 2011), by Matthew M. Hurley of Indiana University Bloomington, Daniel C. Dennett (a prominent philosopher at Tufts University) and Reginal Adams, Jr., of Pennsylvania State University. The book grew out of ideas proposed by Hurley.

Hurley was interested, he wrote on his website, in a contradiction. "Humor is related to some kind of mistake. Every pun, joke and comic incident seemed to contain a fool of some sort—the 'butt' of the joke," he explained. And the typical response is enjoyment of the idiocy—

which "makes sense when it is your enemy or your competition that is somehow failing but not when it is yourself or your loved ones." This observation led him to ask, "Why do we enjoy mistakes?" and to propose that it is not the mistakes per se that people enjoy. It is the "emotional reward for discovering and thus undoing mistakes in thought. We don't enjoy *making* the mistakes, we enjoy weeding them out."

Hurley's thesis is that our mind continuously makes rule-of-thumb conjectures about what will be experienced next and about the intentions of others. The idea is that humor evolved from this constant process of confirmation: people derive amusement from finding discrepancies between expectations and reality when the discrepancies are harmless, and this pleasure keeps us looking for such discrepancies. (To wit: "I was wondering why the Frisbee was getting bigger, and then it hit me.") Moreover, laughter is a public sign of our ability to recognize discrepancies. It is a sign that elevates our social status and allows us to attract reproductive partners.

In other words, a joke is to the sense of humor what a cannoli (loaded with fat and sugar) is to the sense of taste. It is a "supernormal" stimulus that triggers a burst of sensual pleasure—in this case, as a result of spotting mistakes. And because grasping the incongruities requires a store of knowledge and beliefs, shared laughter signals a commonality of worldviews, preferences and convictions, which reinforces social ties and the sense of belonging to the same group. As Hurly told psychologist Jarrett in 2013, the theory goes beyond predicting what makes people laugh. It also explains humor's cognitive value and role in survival.

And yet, as Greengross noted in a review of *Inside Jokes*, even this theory is incomplete. It answers some questions, but it leaves others unresolved—for example, "Why does our appreciation of humor and enjoyment change depending on our mood or other situational conditions?"

Giovannantonio Forabosco, a psychologist and an editor at an Italian journal devoted to studies of humor (*Rivista Italiana di Studi sull'Umorismo*, or *RISU*), agrees: "We certainly haven't heard the last word," he says.

Unanswered Questions

Other questions remain. For instance, how can the sometimes opposite functions of humor, such as promoting social bonding and excluding others with derision, be reconciled? And when laughter enhances feelings of social connectedness, is that effect a fundamental function of the laughter or a mere by-product of some other primary role (much as eating with people has undeniable social value even though eating is primarily motivated by the need for nourishment)?

There is much evidence for a fundamental function. Robert Provine of the University of Maryland, Baltimore County, showed in *Current Directions in Psychological Science*, for example, that individuals laugh 30 times more in the company of others than they do alone. In his research, he and his students surreptitiously observed spontaneous laughter as people went about their business in settings ranging from the student union to shopping malls.

Forabosco notes that there is also some confusion about the relation between humor and laughter: "Laughter is a more social phenomenon, and it occurs for reasons other than humor, including unpleasant ones. Moreover, humor does not always make us laugh." He notes the cases where a person is denigrated or where an observation seems amusing but does not lead to laughter.

A further lingering area of debate concerns humor's role in sexual attraction and thus reproductive success. In one view, knowing how to be funny is a sign of a healthy brain and of good genes, and consequently it attracts partners. Researchers have found that men are more likely to be funny and women are more likely to appreciate a good sense of humor, which is to say that men compete for attention and women do the choosing. But views, of course, differ on this point.

Even the validity of seeking a unified theory of humor is debated. "It is presumptuous to think about cracking the secret of humor with a unified theory," Forabosco says. "We understand many aspects of it, and now the neurosciences are helping to clarify important issues. But as for its essence, it's like saying, 'Let's define the essence of love.' We can study it from many different angles; we can measure the effect of the sight of the beloved on a lover's heart rate. But that doesn't explain love. It's the same with humor. In fact, I always refer to it by describing it, never by defining it."

Still, certain commonalities are now accepted by almost all scholars who study humor. One, Forabosco notes, is a cognitive element: perception of incongruity. "That's necessary but not sufficient," he says, "because there are incongruities that aren't funny. So we have to see what other elements are involved. To my mind, for example, the incongruity needs to be relieved without being totally resolved; it must remain ambiguous, something strange that is never fully explained."

Other cognitive and psychological elements can also provide some punch. These, Forabosco says, include features such as aggression, sexuality, sadism and cynicism. They don't have to be there, but the funniest jokes are those in which they are. Similarly, people tend to see the most humor in jokes that are "very intelligent and very wicked."

"What is humor? Maybe in 40 years we'll know," Forabosco says. And perhaps in 40 years we'll be able to explain why he laughs as he says it.

Referenced

"Laughing, Tickling, and the Evolution of Speech and Self." Robert R. Provine in *Current Directions in Psychological Science*, Vol. 13, No. 6, pages 215–218; December 2004.

"The Evolution and Functions of Laughter and Humor: A Synthetic Approach." Matthew Gervais and David Sloan Wilson in *Quarterly Review of Biology*, Vol. 80, No. 4; pages 395–430; December 2005.

"Benign Violations: Making Immoral Behavior Funny." A. Peter McGraw and Caleb Warren in *Psychological Science*, Vol. 21, No.8, pages 1141–1149; August 2010.

"Too Close for Comfort, or Too Far to Care? Finding Humor in Distant Tragedies and Close Mishaps." A. Peter McGraw et al. in *Psychological Science*, Vol. 23, No. 10; pages 1215–1223; October 2012.

"How Many Psychologists Does It Take ... to Explain a Joke?" Christian Jarrett in *The Psychologist*, Vol. 26, pages 254–259; April 2013.

About the Author

Giovanni Sabato trained as a biologist and is now a freelance science writer based in Rome. Beyond psychology, biology and medicine, he is interested in the links between science and human rights.

How Old Can Humans Get?

By Bill Gifford

How long can human beings live? Although life expectancy has increased significantly over the past century, thanks largely to improved sanitation and medicine, research into hunter-gatherer populations suggests that individuals who escaped disease and violent deaths could live to about their seventh or eighth decade. This means our typical human life span may be static: around 70 years, with an extra decade or so for advanced medical care and cautious behavior. Some geneticists believe a hard limit of around 115 years is essentially programmed into our genome by evolution.

Other scientists in the fast-moving field of aging research, or geroscience, think we can live much longer. A handful of compounds have been shown to lengthen the life spans of laboratory animals slightly, yet some scientists are more ambitious—a lot more ambitious.

João Pedro de Magalhães, a professor of molecular biogerontology at the Institute of Inflammation and Ageing at the University of Birmingham in England, thinks humans could live for 1,000 years. He has scrutinized the genomes of very long-lived animals such as the bowhead whale (which can reach 200 years) and the naked mole rat. His surprising conclusion: if we eliminated aging at the cellular level, humans could live for a millennium—and potentially as long as 20,000 years.

How can that be? If aging is programmed, scientists could theoretically reprogram our cells by tweaking genes that are central to aging. This would require technology that we don't presently have, but Magalhães thinks it can be created. His great-grandfather died of pneumonia—a leading cause of mortality in the 1920s. When Magalhães contracted the same disease as a child, he was cured with a simple dose of penicillin. He thinks scientists can similarly develop therapies for aging, an endeavor to which he has now devoted his career. "I want to cheat death," he says bluntly.

Section 3: Health and the Mind

[An edited transcript of the interview follows.]

Q: How has cheating death worked out so far?
A: I don't think we're going to have a drug that "cures" aging the way penicillin cures infections anytime soon. But a compound called rapamycin is quite promising. It extends lifespan by 10 to 15 percent in animals, and it is approved for human use, such as for organ transplant recipients. It does have side effects. I am optimistic that we will develop drugs akin to statins [taken daily to lessen risk of heart disease] that we take every day for longevity purposes. If you could slow down human aging 10 or even 5 percent, that would still be pretty amazing.

Q: How does rapamycin work?
A: Rapamycin does quite a number of things in the cell, but a lot of its effects [involve] slowing down growth and slowing down cell metabolism, which is why it has an impact on aging.

Q: Your grandmother lived to be 103 years old. Did she take rapamycin, or was her long life linked to something else?
A: I think it was the sun and the beach [*laughs*]. We know that to become a centenarian is mostly genetic. My grandmother didn't really exercise, and she didn't eat very healthily. She didn't smoke; she didn't have very bad habits, but she also didn't have particularly healthy habits. Yet she was quite healthy almost until the end—she was barely in hospital. With her it came down to genetics, environment and some luck.

Q: You've sequenced genomes of very long-lived animals such as the bowhead whale, which lives up to 200 years. How are their genes different from ours, and what can we learn from them?
A: Various long-lived animals, such as humans, whales and elephants, all have to cope with the same issues, such as cancer, but they

use different molecular tricks to achieve their longevity. With bowhead whales, they seem to have much better DNA repair. My dream experiment is to take a bowhead whale gene and implant it in a mouse to see if the mouse would then live longer. Another obvious example would be the *p53* gene, which is very strongly associated with cancer suppression. Elephants have multiple copies of this gene, which makes them resistant to cancer. There are a few other candidate genes that we've discovered, not only in whales but in rodents such as the naked mole rat.

Q: Why are naked mole rats so interesting?
A: Naked mole rats are fascinating because they can live up to 30 years, yet they are smaller than a rat, which only lives to about four years. So you have a small rodent that's related to mice and rats but lives much longer and is very cancer-resistant.

Q: What's their secret?
A: In terms of cancer resistance and probably overall aging as well, it's their ability to respond to and repair DNA damage. But the threshold for a mouse cell to become a cancer cell is much lower than [the threshold] in humans. If you expose mouse cells to DNA damage, they will get cancer; if you expose naked mole rat cells to the same damage, it's going to be fixed. They won't get cancer.

Q: So if mice live several years, and naked mole rats live 30 years, and we live about 80 years, does that mean life spans are genetically programmed?
A: The dominant theory of aging was about wear and tear—damage accumulating in our cells and components of our body like cars that break down over time. I've never really liked that because humans are not inanimate objects. There *is* damage, of course, and often aging seems to be very deterministic, almost like a program. A mouse will age 20 to 30 times faster than a human being. There are a lot of aging [characteristics] that just happen

to everybody and even across species, such as loss of muscle mass. This doesn't seem like something that's random; it seems predetermined. So I think of aging as more akin to a software problem than a hardware problem.

My hypothesis is that we have a very complicated set of computerlike programs in our DNA that turn us into an adult human being. But maybe some of these same programs, as they continue into later life, become detrimental.

Q: What's an example of that?
A: A classic example would be thymus involution. Your thymus is a gland that produces T cells, which are very important to your immune system. But it disappears fairly early in life, around age 20—earlier if you're obese; later if you're an athlete. Basically it turns into fat. That strikes me as very programmatic. It's a classic case of antagonistic pleiotropy, where a process that is beneficial earlier in life becomes harmful later on.

Q: Why is the immune system important in aging?
A: The immune system, I think, is a low-hanging fruit in terms of targeting aging. It has systemic impacts, and it declines over time, which is why diseases like COVID become very dangerous to old people. But there are specific tissues, such as the thymus, that you can target for rejuvenation. To me, that's one way of starting. There are experiments in mice that show that if you change just one transcription factor [a protein that acts on genetic material], the thymus regenerates. In theory, I am convinced we can have radical interventions like this—to rewrite our genetic "software" and redesign human biology—to delay or even reverse aging. In practice, it is difficult, but in theory, I think there's a huge potential.

Q: How much potential is there? How long could we live if we got rid of aging?

A: I actually did some calculations years ago and found that if we could "cure" human aging, average human life span would be more than 1,000 years. Maximum life span, barring accidents and violent death, could be as long as 20,000 years. This may sound like a lot, but some species can already live hundreds of years—and in some cases thousands of years [such as the hexactinellid sponge and the Great Basin bristlecone pine]. If we could redesign our biology to eliminate cancer and evade the detrimental actions of our genetic software program, the health benefits would be mind-boggling.

Q: This sounds extreme. Are such profound interventions even possible?
A: I think it's possible. Is it going to happen soon? I think it's quite unlikely. Even if you can figure out how aging works, it is not easy to develop interventions. I am an aspiring science-fiction writer as well, and one thing I've noticed are these novels that are set 100 or 1,000 years from now, in a future with all kinds of technology that enables people to do incredible things, such as travel between stars—and people are still aging. But I think we'll figure out aging by then.

About the Author

Bill Gifford is co-author of the New York Times *bestseller* Outlive: The Science & Art of Longevity. *He ages in Salt Lake City, Utah.*

Section 4: Human Nature

4.1 What's the World's Oldest Language?
By Lucy Tu

4.2 War Is *Not* Part of Human Nature
By R. Brian Ferguson

4.3 Is Inequality Inevitable?
By Bruce M. Boghosian

4.4 The Theory That Men Evolved to Hunt and Women Evolved to Gather Is Wrong
By Cara Ocobock & Sarah Lacy

What's the World's Oldest Language?

By Lucy Tu

The globe hums with thousands of languages. But when did humans first lay out a structured system to communicate, one that was distinct to a particular area?

Scientists are aware of more than 7,100 languages in use today. Nearly 40 percent of them are considered endangered, meaning they have a declining number of speakers and are at risk of dying out. Some languages are spoken by fewer than 1,000 people, while more than half of the world's population uses one of just 23 tongues.

These languages and dead ones that are no longer spoken weave together millennia of human interactions. That means the task of determining the world's oldest language is more than a linguistic curiosity. For instance, in order to decipher clay tablet inscriptions or trace the evolution of living tongues, linguists must grapple with questions that extend beyond language. In doing so, their research reveals some of the secrets of ancient civilizations and even sparks debates that blend science and culture.

"Ancient languages, just like contemporary languages, are crucial for understanding the past. We can trace the history of human migrations and contacts through languages. And in some cases, the language information is our only reliable source of information about the past," says Claire Bowern, a Professor of Linguistics at Yale University. "The words that we can trace back through time give us a picture of the culture of past societies."

Language comes in different forms—including speech, gestures and writing—which don't all leave conclusive evidence behind. And experts use different approaches to determine a language's age.

Tracing the oldest language is "a deceptively complicated task," says Danny Hieber, a linguist who studies endangered languages. One way to identify a language's origins is to find the point at which a single tongue with different dialects became two entirely distinct languages, such that people speaking those dialects could no longer understand each other. "For example, how far back in history would you need to go for English speakers to understand German speakers?" he says. That point in time would mark the origins of English and German as distinct languages, branching off from a common proto-Germanic language.

Alternatively, if we assume that most languages can be traced back to an original, universal human language, all languages are equally old. "You know that your parents spoke a language, and their parents spoke a language, and so forth. So intuitively, you'd imagine that all languages were born from a single origin," Hieber says.

But it's impossible to prove the existence of a proto-human language—the hypothetical direct ancestor of every language in the world. Accordingly, some linguists argue that the designation of the "oldest language" should belong to one with a well-established written record.

Many of the earliest documented examples of writing come from languages that used cuneiform script, which featured wedge-shaped characters impressed into clay tablets. Among these languages are Sumerian and Akkadian, both dating back at least 4,600 years. Archaeologists have also found Egyptian hieroglyphs carved into the tomb of Pharaoh Seth-Peribsen that date to around the same historical period. The inscription translates to: "He has united the Two Lands for his son, Dual King Peribsen," and it is considered the earliest-known complete sentence.

Historians and linguists generally agree that Sumerian, Akkadian and Egyptian are the oldest languages with a clear written record. All three are extinct, meaning they are no longer used and do not have any living descendants that can carry the language to the next generation.

As for the oldest language that is still spoken, several contenders emerge. Hebrew and Arabic stand out among such languages for having timelines that linguists can reasonably trace, according to Hieber. Although the earliest written evidence of these languages dates back only around 3,000 years, Hieber says that both belong to the Afroasiatic language family, whose roots trace back to 18,000 to 8,000 B.C.E., or about 20,000 to 10,000 years ago. Even with this broad time frame, contemporary linguists widely accept Afroasiatic as the oldest language family. But the exact point at which Hebrew and Arabic diverged from other Afroasiatic languages is heavily disputed.

Bowern adds Chinese to the list of candidates. The language likely emerged from Proto-Sino-Tibetan, which is also an ancestor to Burmese and the Tibetan languages, around 4,500 years ago, although the exact date is disputed. The earliest documented evidence of the Chinese writing system comes from inscriptions on tortoise shells and animal bones that date back to about 3,300 years ago. Modern Chinese characters weren't introduced until centuries later, however.

Turn the clock back an additional one or two millennia, and the linguistic record becomes especially murky. Deven Patel, a professor of South Asia studies at the University of Pennsylvania, says the earliest written records of Sanskrit are ancient Hindu texts that were composed between 1500 and 1200 B.C.E. and are part of the Vedas, a collection of religious works from ancient India. "In my view, Sanskrit is the oldest continuous language tradition, meaning it's still producing literature and people speak it, although it's not a first language in the modern era," Patel says.

Some linguists, however, argue that the appearance of Sanskrit was predated by Tamil, a Dravidian language that is still used by almost 85 million native speakers in southern India and Sri Lanka. Scientists have documented Tamil for at least 2,000 years. But scholars have contested the true age of the oldest surviving work of Tamil literature, known as the *Tolkāppiyam*, with estimates ranging from 7,000 to 2,800 years. "There are disputes among scholars about the precise date of ancient texts ascribed to Tamil and whether the language used is actually similar enough to modern Tamil to categorize them as the same language," Patel says. "Tamil [speakers] have been especially [enthusiastic] in trying to separate the language as uniquely ancient."

Disagreements about the age of Sanskrit and Tamil illustrate the broader issues in pinpointing the world's oldest language. "To answer this question, we've seen people create new histories, which are as much political as they are scientific," Patel says. "There are bragging rights associated with being the oldest and still evolving language."

About the Author

Lucy Tu is a freelance writer and a Rhodes Scholar studying reproductive medicine and law. She was a 2023 AAAS Mass Media Fellow at Scientific American.

War Is *Not* Part of Human Nature

By R. Brian Ferguson

Do people, or perhaps just males, have an evolved predisposition to kill members of other groups? Not just a capacity to kill but an innate propensity to take up arms, tilting us toward collective violence? The word "collective" is key. People fight and kill for personal reasons, but homicide is not war. War is social, with groups organized to kill people from other groups. Today controversy over the historical roots of warfare revolves around two polar positions. In one, war is an evolved propensity to eliminate any potential competitors. In this scenario, humans all the way back to our common ancestors with chimpanzees have always made war. The other position holds that armed conflict has only emerged over recent millennia, as changing social conditions provided the motivation and organization to collectively kill. The two sides separate into what the late anthropologist Keith Otterbein called hawks and doves. (This debate also ties into the question of whether instinctive, warlike tendencies can be detected in chimpanzees [*see sidebar on pages 110–111*].)

If war expresses an inborn tendency, then we should expect to find evidence of war in small-scale societies throughout the prehistoric record. The hawks claim that we have indeed found such evidence. "When there is a good archaeological picture of any society on Earth, there is almost always also evidence of warfare.... Twenty-five percent of deaths due to warfare may be a conservative estimate," wrote archaeologist Steven A. LeBlanc and his co-author Katherine E. Register. With casualties of that magnitude, evolutionary psychologists argue, war has served as a mechanism of natural selection in which the fittest prevail to acquire both mates and resources.

This perspective has achieved broad influence. Political scientist Francis Fukuyama wrote that the roots of recent wars and genocide go back for tens or hundreds of thousands of years among our hunter-gatherer ancestors, even to our shared ancestor with chimpanzees. Bradley Thayer, a leading scholar of international relations, argues that evolutionary theory explains why the instinctual tendency to protect one's tribe morphed over time into group inclinations toward xenophobia and ethnocentrism in international relations. If wars are natural eruptions of instinctive hate, why look for other answers? If human nature leans toward collective killing of outsiders, how long can we avoid it?

The anthropologists and archaeologists in the dove camp challenge this view. Humans, they argue, have an obvious capacity to engage in warfare, but their brains are not hardwired to identify and kill outsiders involved in collective conflicts. Lethal group attacks, according to these arguments, emerged only when hunter-gatherer societies grew in size and complexity and later with the birth of agriculture. Archaeology, supplemented by observations of contemporary hunter-gatherer cultures, allows us to identify the times and, to some degree, the social circumstances that led to the origins and intensification of warfare.

When Did It Begin?

In the search for the origins of war, archaeologists look for four kinds of evidence. The artwork on cave walls is exhibit one. Paleolithic cave paintings from Grottes de Cougnac, Pech Merle and Cosquer in France dating back approximately 25,000 years show what some scholars perceive to be spears penetrating people, suggesting that people were waging war as early as the late Paleolithic period. But this interpretation is contested. Other scientists point out that some of the incomplete figures in those cave paintings have tails, and they argue that the bent or wavy lines that intersect with them more likely represent forces of shamanic power, not spears. (In contrast, wall paintings on the eastern Iberian Peninsula, probably made by settled agriculturalists thousands of years later, clearly show battles and executions.)

Weapons are also evidence of war, but these artifacts may not be what they seem. I used to accept maces as representing proof of war, until I learned more about Near Eastern stone maces. Most have holes for handles so narrow they could not survive one blow in battle. Maces also symbolize authority, and established rule can provide a way to resolve conflict without resorting to war. On the other hand, it is perfectly possible to go to war *without* traditional weapons: in southern Germany around 5000 B.C., villagers were massacred with adzes that were also used to work wood.

Beyond art and weapons, archaeologists look to settlement remains for clues. People who fear attack usually take precautions. In the archaeological record, we sometimes see people who lived in scattered homes on low flatlands shifted to nucleated defendable villages. Villages across Neolithic Europe were surrounded by mounded enclosures. But not all these enclosures seem designed for defense. Some may mark off distinct social groups.

Skeletal remains would seem ideal for determining when war began, but even these require careful assessment. Only one of three or four projectile wounds leaves a mark on bone. Shaped points made of stone or bone buried with a corpse are sometimes ceremonial, sometimes the cause of death. Unhealed wounds to a single buried corpse could be the result of an accident, an execution or a homicide. Indeed, homicide may have been fairly common in the prehistoric world—but homicide is not war. And not all fights were lethal. In some burial sites, archaeologists frequently find skulls with healed cranial depressions but few that caused death. The findings suggest fights with clubs or other nonlethal resolution of personal disputes, as is common in the ethnographic record. When the skulls are mostly from females, fractures may reflect domestic violence.

The global archaeological evidence, then, is often ambiguous and difficult to interpret. Often different clues must be pieced together to produce a suspicion or probability of war. But dedicated archaeological work—multiple excavations with good material recovery—should be able to conclude that war is at least suspected.

On balance, though, are there really indications that humans have been waging war for the entire history of the species? If your sample consists of cases known for high frequencies of perimortem wounds (those occurring at or near the time of death), the situation looks pretty bad. That is how figures such as 25 percent of deaths by violence are derived. Misconceptions result, however, because of cherry-picking by popular media. Any discovery of ancient killings grabs headlines. The news items ignore innumerable excavations that yield no signs of violence. And a comprehensive screening of reports from a particular area and time period, asking how many, if any, show even hints of war, paints an entirely different picture. War is hardly ubiquitous and does not go back endlessly in the archaeological record. Human warfare did indeed have a beginning.

The First Hostilities

Many archaeologists venture that war emerged in some areas during the Mesolithic period, which began after the last Ice Age ended around 9700 B.C., when European hunter-gatherers settled and developed more complex societies. But there really is no simple answer. War appeared at different times in different places. For half a century archaeologists have agreed that the multiple violent deaths at Jebel Sahaba along the Nile in northern Sudan occurred even earlier, around 12,000 B.C. There severe competition among settled hunter-gatherer groups in an area with once rich but declining food sources may have led to conflict.

At a slightly later time, settlements, weapons and burials in the northern Tigris suggest war involving settled villages of hunter-gatherers between 9750 and 8750 B.C. Nearby, the earliest known village fortifications occurred among farming people in the seventh millennium, and the first conquest of an urban center took place between 3800 and 3500 B.C. By that date, war was common across Anatolia, spread in part by conquering migrants from the northern Tigris.

In stark contrast, archaeologists have found no persuasive evidence in settlements, weapons or skeletal remains in the southern Levant (from Sinai to southern Lebanon and Syria) dating to before about

3200 B.C. In Japan, violent deaths from any cause are rare among hunter-gatherer groups from 13,000 to 800 B.C.

With the development of wet rice farming around 300 B.C., violent fatalities became apparent in more than one in 10 remains. In well-studied North American sites, some very early skeletal trauma seems the result of personal rather than collective conflicts. A site in Florida contained evidence of multiple killings about 5400 B.C. In parts of the Pacific Northwest, the same occurred by 2200 B.C., but in the southern Great Plains, only one violent death was recorded before A.D. 500.

Why Did It Happen?

The preconditions that make war more likely include a shift to a more sedentary existence, a growing regional population, a concentration of valuable resources such as livestock, increasing social complexity and hierarchy, trade in high-value goods, and the establishment of group boundaries and collective identities. These conditions are sometimes combined with severe environmental changes. War at Jebel Sahaba, for one, may have been a response to an ecological crisis, as the Nile cut a gorge that eliminated productive marshlands, eventually leading to human abandonment of the area. Later, centuries after agriculture began, Neolithic Europe—to take one example—demonstrated that when people have more to fight over, their societies start to organize themselves in a manner that makes them more prepared to go ahead and embrace war.

There are limits, however, to what archaeology can show, and we must seek answers elsewhere. Ethnography—the study of different cultures, both living and past—illustrates these preconditions. A basic distinction is between "simple" and "complex" hunter-gatherer communities.

Simple hunting and gathering characterized human societies during most of humanity's existence dating back more than 200,000 years. Broadly, these groups cooperate with one another and live in small, mobile, egalitarian bands, exploiting large areas with low population density and few possessions.

Complex hunter-gatherers, in contrast, live in fixed settlements with populations in the hundreds. They maintain social rankings of kin groups and individuals, restrict access to food resources by lines of descent and have more developed political leadership. Signs of such social complexity first appeared during the Mesolithic. The appearance of complex hunter-gatherers can sometimes but not always mark a transitional stage to agriculture, the basis for the development of political states. These groups, moreover, often waged war.

The preconditions for war are only part of the story, however, and by themselves, they may not suffice to predict outbreaks of collective conflicts. In the Southern Levant, for instance, those preconditions existed for thousands of years without evidence of war.

Why, though, was there an absence of conflict? It turns out that many societies also have distinct preconditions for peace. Many social arrangements impede war, such as cross-group ties of kinship and marriage; cooperation in hunting, agriculture or food sharing; flexibility in social arrangements that allow individuals to move to other groups; norms that value peace and stigmatize killing; and recognized means for conflict resolution. These mechanisms do not eliminate serious conflict, but they do channel it in ways that either prevent killing or keep it confined among a limited number of individuals.

If this is so, why then are later archaeological findings, along with explorers' and anthropologists' reports, so full of deadly warfare? Over millennia preconditions of war became more common in more places. Once established, war has a tendency to spread, with violent peoples replacing less violent ones. States evolved around the world, and states are capable of militarizing peoples on their peripheries and trade routes. Environmental upheavals such as frequent droughts aggravate and sometimes generate conditions that lead to war, and peace may not return when conditions ease. Particularly notable was the intensification of the Medieval Warm period, from roughly A.D. 950 to 1250, and its rapid transformation into the Little Ice Age beginning around A.D. 1300. In that period war increased in areas across the Americas, the Pacific and elsewhere. In most of the world, war was long established, but conflicts worsened, with mounting casualties tallied.

Then came European global expansion, which transformed, intensified and sometimes generated indigenous war around the world. These confrontations were not just driven by conquest and resistance. Local peoples began to make war on one another, drawn into new hostilities by colonial powers and the commodities they provided.

Interaction between ancient and recent expanding states, and the ensuing conflicts, encouraged formation of distinctive tribal identities and divisions. Areas still beyond colonial control underwent changes impelled by longer-distance effects of trade, disease and population displacement—all of which led to wars. States also stirred up conflict among local peoples by imposing political institutions with clear boundaries rather than the amorphous local identities and limited authorities they often encountered in their colonial forays.

Scholars often seek support for the idea that human willingness to engage in deadly group hostilities predated the rise of the state by looking for evidence of hostilities in "tribal zones," where "savage" warfare seems endemic and is often seen as an expression of human nature. But a careful examination of ethnographically known violence among local peoples in the historical record provides an alternative perspective.

Hunter-gatherers of northwestern Alaska from the late 18th through the 19th centuries demonstrate the fallacy of projecting ethnography of contemporary peoples into humanity's distant past. Intense war involving village massacres lingers in detailed oral traditions. This deadly violence is cited as evidence of war by hunter-gatherers before disruption by expanding states.

Archaeology, however, combined with the history of the region, provides a very different assessment. There are no hints of war in early archaeological remains in the simple cultures of Alaskan hunter-gatherers. The first signs of war appear between A.D. 400 to 700, and they are probably the result of contact with immigrants from Asia or southern Alaska, where war was already established. But these conflicts were limited in size and probably intensity.

With favorable climatic conditions by A.D. 1200, a growing social complexity developed among these whale hunters, with denser, more settled populations and expanding long-distance trade. After a couple of centuries, war became common. War in the 19th century, however, was much worse, so severe that it caused decline of the regional population. These later conflicts—the ones that show up in oral histories—were associated with state expansion as a massive trade network developed out of new Russian entrepôts in Siberia, and they led to extreme territoriality and centralization of complex tribal groups across the Bering Strait.

Not a Fact of Life

Debate over war and human nature will not soon be resolved. The idea that intensive, high-casualty violence was ubiquitous throughout prehistory has many backers. It has cultural resonance for those who are sure that we as a species naturally tilt toward war. As my mother would say: "Just look at history!" But doves have the upper hand when all the evidence is considered. Broadly, early finds provide little if any evidence suggesting war was a fact of life.

People are people. They fight and sometimes kill. Humans have always had a capacity to make war, if conditions and culture so dictate. But those conditions and the warlike cultures they generate became common only over the past 10,000 years—and, in most places, much more recently than that. The high level of killing often reported in history, ethnography or later archaeology is contradicted in the earliest archaeological findings around the globe. The most ancient bones and artifacts are consistent with the title of Margaret Mead's 1940 article: "Warfare Is Only an Invention—Not a Biological Necessity."

What about Our Chimp Cousins?

Delving into the question of human predisposition to war often involves looking beyond our species to examine the experiences of our chimpanzee relatives. This is a topic I have been studying for many years, and I am now finishing the writing of a book about it, *Chimpanzees, "War," and History*. I put quotes around "war" because intergroup conflict among chimps, though sometimes collective and deadly, lacks the social and cognitive dimensions essential to human war.

Human warfare involves opponents that often include multiple local groups that may be unified by widely varying forms of political organization. War is fostered by culturally specific systems of knowledge and values that generate powerful meanings of "us versus them." These social constructs have no primate analogies. Despite these distinctions, some scientists have argued that chimpanzees demonstrate an innate propensity to kill outsiders, inherited from the last common ancestor of chimps and people—an impulse that still subliminally pushes humans as well into deadly conflicts with those outside their communities.

My work disputes the claim that chimpanzee males have an innate tendency to kill outsiders, arguing instead that their most extreme violence can be tied to specific circumstances that result from disruption of their lives by contact with humans. Making that case has required my going through every reported chimpanzee killing. From this, a simple point can be made. Critical examination of a recent compilation of killings from 18 chimpanzee research sites—together amounting to 426 years of field observations—reveals that of 27 observed or inferred intergroup killings of adults and adolescents, 15 come from just two highly conflicted situations, which occurred at two sites in 1974–1977 and 2002–2006, respectively.

The two situations amount to nine years of observation, tallying a kill rate of 1.67 annually for those years. The remaining 417 years of observation average just 0.03 annually. The question is whether the outlier cases are better explained as evolved, adaptive behavior or as a result of human disruption. And whereas some evolutionary biologists propose that killings are explained as attempts to diminish the number of males in rival groups, those same data show that subtracting internal from external killings of males produces a reduction of outside males of only one every 47 years, fewer than once in a chimpanzee's lifetime.

From comparative case studies, I conclude that "war" among chimpanzees is not an evolved evolutionary strategy but an induced response to human disturbance. Case-by-case analyses will show that chimps, as a species, are not "killer apes." This research calls into question as well the idea that any human tendency toward bellicosity might be driven by an ancient genetic legacy from a distant ancestor of chimpanzees and humans.

—R.B.F.

Referenced

War in the Tribal Zone: Expanding States and Indigenous Warfare. Edited by R. Brian Ferguson and Neil L. Whitehead. School of American Research Press, 1992.

Beyond War: The Human Potential for Peace. Douglas P. Fry. Oxford University Press, 2007.

About the Author

R. Brian Ferguson is a professor of anthropology at Rutgers University–Newark. His academic career has been devoted to explaining why war happens.

Is Inequality Inevitable?

By Bruce M. Boghosian

Wealth inequality is escalating at an alarming rate not only within the U.S. but also in countries as diverse as Russia, India and Brazil. According to investment bank Credit Suisse, the fraction of global household wealth held by the richest 1 percent of the world's population increased from 42.5 to 47.2 percent between the financial crisis of 2008 and 2018. To put it another way, as of 2010, 388 individuals possessed as much household wealth as the lower half of the world's population combined—about 3.5 billion people; today Oxfam estimates that number as 26. Statistics from almost all nations that measure wealth in their household surveys indicate that it is becoming increasingly concentrated.

Although the origins of inequality are hotly debated, an approach developed by physicists and mathematicians, including my group at Tufts University, suggests they have long been hiding in plain sight—in a well-known quirk of arithmetic. This method uses models of wealth distribution collectively known as agent-based, which begin with an individual transaction between two "agents" or actors, each trying to optimize his or her own financial outcome. In the modern world, nothing could seem more fair or natural than two people deciding to exchange goods, agreeing on a price and shaking hands. Indeed, the seeming stability of an economic system arising from this balance of supply and demand among individual actors is regarded as a pinnacle of Enlightenment thinking—to the extent that many people have come to conflate the free market with the notion of freedom itself. Our deceptively simple mathematical models, which are based on voluntary transactions, suggest, however, that it is time for a serious reexamination of this idea.

In particular, the affine wealth model (called thus because of its mathematical properties) can describe wealth distribution among households in diverse developed countries with exquisite precision while revealing a subtle asymmetry that tends to concentrate wealth.

We believe that this purely analytical approach, which resembles an x-ray in that it is used not so much to represent the messiness of the real world as to strip it away and reveal the underlying skeleton, provides deep insight into the forces acting to increase poverty and inequality today.

Oligarchy

In 1986 social scientist John Angle first described the movement and distribution of wealth as arising from pairwise transactions among a collection of "economic agents," which could be individuals, households, companies, funds or other entities. By the turn of the century physicists Slava Ispolatov, Pavel L. Krapivsky and Sidney Redner, then all working together at Boston University, as well as Adrian Drăgulescu, now at Constellation Energy Group, and Victor Yakovenko of the University of Maryland, had demonstrated that these agent-based models could be analyzed with the tools of statistical physics, leading to rapid advances in our understanding of their behavior. As it turns out, many such models find wealth moving inexorably from one agent to another—even if they are based on fair exchanges between equal actors. In 2002 Anirban Chakraborti, then at the Saha Institute of Nuclear Physics in Kolkata, India, introduced what came to be known as the yard sale model, called thus because it has certain features of real one-on-one economic transactions. He also used numerical simulations to demonstrate that it inexorably concentrated wealth, resulting in oligarchy.

To understand how this happens, suppose you are in a casino and are invited to play a game. You must place some ante—say, $100—on a table, and a fair coin will be flipped. If the coin comes up heads, the house will pay you 20 percent of what you have on the table, resulting in $120 on the table. If the coin comes up tails, the house will take 17 percent of what you have on the table, resulting in $83 left on the table. You can keep your money on the table for as many flips of the coin as you would like (without ever adding to or subtracting from it). Each time you play, you will win

20 percent of what is on the table if the coin comes up heads, and you will lose 17 percent of it if the coin comes up tails. Should you agree to play this game?

You might construct two arguments, both rather persuasive, to help you decide what to do. You may think, "I have a probability of ½ of gaining $20 and a probability of ½ of losing $17. My expected gain is therefore:

$$½ \times (\$20) + ½ \times (-\$17) = \$1.50$$

which is positive. In other words, my odds of winning and losing are even, but my gain if I win will be greater than my loss if I lose." From this perspective it seems advantageous to play this game.

Or, like a chess player, you might think further: "What if I stay for 10 flips of the coin? A likely outcome is that five of them will come up heads and that the other five will come up tails. Each time heads comes up, my ante is multiplied by 1.2. Each time tails comes up, my ante is multiplied by 0.83. After five wins and five losses in any order, the amount of money remaining on the table will be:

$$1.2 \times 1.2 \times 1.2 \times 1.2 \times 1.2 \times 0.83 \times 0.83 \times 0.83 \times 0.83 \times 0.83 \times \$100 = \$98.02$$

so I will have lost about $2 of my original $100 ante." With a bit more work you can confirm that it would take about 93 wins to compensate for 91 losses. From this perspective it seems disadvantageous to play this game.

The contradiction between the two arguments presented here may seem surprising at first, but it is well known in probability and finance. Its connection with wealth inequality is less familiar, however. To extend the casino metaphor to the movement of wealth in an (exceedingly simplified) economy, let us imagine a system of 1,000 individuals who engage in pairwise exchanges with one another. Let each begin with some initial wealth, which could be exactly equal. Choose two agents at random and have them transact, then do the same with another two, and so on. In other words, this model assumes sequential transactions between randomly chosen pairs of agents.

Our plan is to conduct millions or billions of such transactions in our population of 1,000 and see how the wealth ultimately gets distributed.

What should a single transaction between a pair of agents look like? People have a natural aversion to going broke, so we assume that the amount at stake, which we call $\Delta\omega$ ($\Delta\omega$ is pronounced "delta w"), is a mere fraction of the wealth of the poorer person, Shauna. That way, even if Shauna loses in a transaction with Eric, the richer person, the amount she loses is always less than her own total wealth. This is not an unreasonable assumption and in fact captures a self-imposed limitation that most people instinctively observe in their economic life. To begin with—just because these numbers are familiar to us—let us suppose $\Delta\omega$ is 20 percent of Shauna's wealth, ω, if she wins and -17 percent of ω if she loses. (Our actual model assumes that the win and loss percentages are equal, but the general outcome still holds. Moreover, increasing or decreasing $\Delta\omega$ will just extend the time scale so that more transactions will be required before we can see the ultimate result, which will remain unaltered.)

If our goal is to model a fair and stable market economy, we ought to begin by assuming that nobody has an advantage of any kind, so let us decide the direction in which ω is moved by the flip of a fair coin. If the coin comes up heads, Shauna gets 20 percent of her wealth from Eric; if the coin comes up tails, she must give 17 percent of it to Eric. Now randomly choose another pair of agents from the total of 1,000 and do it again. In fact, go ahead and do this a million times or a billion times. What happens?

If you simulate this economy, a variant of the yard sale model, you will get a remarkable result: after a large number of transactions, one agent ends up as an "oligarch" holding practically all the wealth of the economy, and the other 999 end up with virtually nothing. It does not matter how much wealth people started with. It does not matter that all the coin flips were absolutely fair. It does not matter that the poorer agent's expected outcome was positive in each transaction, whereas that of the richer agent was negative. Any single agent in this economy could have become the oligarch—in fact, all had equal odds if they began with equal wealth. In that sense, there was equality of opportunity. But only one of them *did* become the oligarch, and all the others saw their average wealth decrease toward zero as they conducted more and more transactions. To add insult to injury, the lower someone's wealth ranking, the faster the decrease.

This outcome is especially surprising because it holds even if all the agents started off with identical wealth and were treated symmetrically. Physicists describe phenomena of this kind as "symmetry breaking." The very first coin flip transfers money from one agent to another, setting up an imbalance between the two. And once we have some variance in wealth, however minute, succeeding transactions will systematically move a "trickle" of wealth upward from poorer agents to richer ones, amplifying inequality until the system reaches a state of oligarchy.

If the economy is unequal to begin with, the poorest agent's wealth will probably decrease the fastest. Where does it go? It must go to wealthier agents because there are no poorer agents. Things are not much better for the second-poorest agent. In the long run, all participants in this economy except for the very richest one will see their wealth decay exponentially. In separate papers in 2015 my colleagues and I at Tufts University and Christophe Chorro of Université Panthéon-Sorbonne provided mathematical proofs of the outcome that Chakraborti's simulations had uncovered—that the yard sale model moves wealth inexorably from one side to the other.

Does this mean that poorer agents never win or that richer agents never lose? Certainly not. Once again, the setup resembles a casino—you win some and you lose some, but the longer you stay in the casino, the more likely you are to lose. The free market is essentially a casino that you can never leave. When the trickle of wealth described earlier, flowing from poor to rich in each transaction, is multiplied by 7.7 billion people in the world conducting countless transactions every year, the trickle becomes a torrent. Inequality inevitably grows more pronounced because of the collective effects of enormous numbers of seemingly innocuous but subtly biased transactions.

Section 4: Human Nature

The Condensation of Wealth

You might, of course, wonder how this model, even if mathematically accurate, has anything to do with reality. After all, it describes an entirely unstable economy that inevitably degenerates to complete oligarchy, and there are no complete oligarchies in the world. It is true that, by itself, the yard sale model is unable to explain empirical wealth distributions. To address this deficiency, my group has refined it in three ways to make it more realistic.

In 2017 Adrian Devitt-Lee, Merek Johnson, Jie Li, Jeremy Marcq, Hongyan Wang and I, all at Tufts, incorporated the redistribution of wealth. In keeping with the simplicity desirable in applied mathematics models, we did this by having each agent take a step toward the mean wealth in the society after each transaction. The size of the step was some fraction χ (or "chi") of his or her distance from the mean. This is equivalent to a flat wealth tax for the wealthy (with tax rate χ per unit time) and a complementary subsidy for the poor. In effect, it transfers wealth from those above the mean to those below it. We found that this simple modification stabilized the wealth distribution so that oligarchy no longer resulted. And astonishingly, it enabled our model to match empirical data on U.S. and European wealth distribution between 1989 and 2016 to better than 2 percent. The single parameter χ seems to subsume a host of real-world taxes and subsidies that would be too messy to include separately in a skeletal model such as this one.

In addition, it is well documented that the wealthy enjoy systemic economic advantages such as lower interest rates on loans and better financial advice, whereas the poor suffer systemic economic disadvantages such as payday lenders and a lack of time to shop for the best prices. As James Baldwin once observed, "Anyone who has ever struggled with poverty knows how extremely expensive it is to be poor." Accordingly, in the same paper mentioned above, we factored in what we call wealth-attained advantage. We biased the coin flip in favor of the wealthier individual by an amount proportional to a new parameter, ζ (or "zeta"), times the wealth difference divided by the mean wealth. This rather simple refinement, which serves as a proxy for a multitude of biases favoring the wealthy, improved agreement between the model and the upper tail of actual wealth distributions.

The inclusion of wealth-related bias also yields—and gives a precise mathematical definition to—the phenomenon of partial oligarchy. Whenever the influence of wealth-attained advantage exceeds that of redistribution (more precisely, whenever ζ exceeds χ), a vanishingly small fraction of people will possess a finite fraction, $1 - \chi/\zeta$, of societal wealth. The onset of partial oligarchy is in fact a phase transition for another model of economic transactions, as first described in 2000 by physicists Jean-Philippe Bouchaud, now at École Polytechnique, and Marc Mézard of the École Normale Supérieure. In our model, when ζ is less than χ, the system has only one stable state with no oligarchy; when ζ exceeds χ, a new, oligarchical state appears and becomes the stable state. The two-parameter (χ and ζ) extended yard sale model thus obtained can match empirical data on U.S. and European wealth distribution between 1989 and 2016 to within 1 to 2 percent.

Such a phase transition may have played a crucial role in the condensation of wealth following the breakup of the Soviet Union in 1991. The imposition of what was called shock therapy economics on the former states of the U.S.S.R. resulted in a dramatic decrease of wealth redistribution (that is, decreasing χ) by their governments and a concomitant jump in wealth-attained advantage (increasing ζ) from the combined effects of sudden privatization and deregulation. The resulting decrease of the "temperature" χ/ζ threw the countries into a wealth-condensed state, so that formerly communist countries became partial oligarchies almost overnight. To the present day at least 10 of the 15 former Soviet republics can be accurately described as oligarchies.

As a third refinement, in 2019 we included negative wealth—one of the more disturbing aspects of modern economies—in our model. In 2016, for example, approximately 10.5 percent of the U.S. population was in net debt because of mortgages, student loans and other factors. So we introduced a third parameter, κ (or "kappa"), which shifts the wealth distribution downward, thereby accounting for negative wealth. We supposed that the least wealth the poorest agent could have at any time was $-S$, where S equals κ times the mean wealth. Prior to each transaction, we loaned wealth S to both agents so that each had positive wealth. They then transacted according to the extended yard sale model, described earlier, after which they both repaid their debt of S.

The three-parameter (χ, ζ, κ) model thus obtained, called the affine wealth model, can match empirical data on U.S. wealth distribution to less than a sixth of a percent over a span of three decades. (In mathematics, the word "affine" describes something that scales multiplicatively and translates additively. In this case, some features of the model, such as the value of Δω, scale multiplicatively with the wealth of the agent, whereas other features, such as the addition or subtraction of S, are additive translations or displacements in "wealth space.") Agreement with European wealth-distribution data for 2010 is typically better than a third to a half of a percent.

To obtain these comparisons with actual data, we had to solve the "inverse problem." That is, given the empirical wealth distribution, we had to find the values of (χ, ζ, κ) at which the results of our model most closely matched it. As just one example, the 2016 U.S. household wealth distribution is best described as having χ = 0.036, ζ = 0.050 and κ = 0.058. The affine wealth model has been applied to empirical data from many countries and epochs. To the best of our knowledge, it describes wealth-distribution data more accurately than any other existing model.

Trickle Up

We find it noteworthy that the best-fitting model for empirical wealth distribution discovered so far is one that would be completely unstable without redistribution rather than one based on a supposed equilibrium of market forces. In fact, these mathematical models demonstrate that far from wealth trickling down to the poor, the natural inclination of wealth is to flow upward, so that the "natural" wealth distribution in a free-market economy is one of complete oligarchy. It is only redistribution that sets limits on inequality.

The mathematical models also call attention to the enormous extent to which wealth distribution is caused by symmetry breaking, chance and early advantage (from, for example, inheritance). And the presence of symmetry breaking puts paid to arguments for the justness of wealth inequality that appeal to "voluntariness"—the notion that individuals bear all responsibility for their economic outcomes simply because they enter into transactions voluntarily—or to the idea that wealth accumulation must be the result of cleverness and industriousness. It is true that an individual's location on the wealth spectrum correlates to some extent with such attributes, but the overall shape of that spectrum can be explained to better than 0.33 percent by a statistical model that completely ignores them. Luck plays a much more important role than it is usually accorded, so that the virtue commonly attributed to wealth in modern society—and, likewise, the stigma attributed to poverty—is completely unjustified.

Moreover, only a carefully designed mechanism for redistribution can compensate for the natural tendency of wealth to flow from the poor to the rich in a market economy. Redistribution is often confused with taxes, but the two concepts ought to be kept quite separate. Taxes flow from people to their governments to finance those governments' activities. Redistribution, in contrast, may be implemented by governments, but it is best thought of as a flow of wealth from people to people to compensate for the unfairness inherent in market economics. In a flat redistribution scheme, all those possessing wealth below the mean would receive net funds, whereas those above the mean would pay. And precisely because current levels of inequality are so extreme, far more people would receive than would pay.

Given how complicated real economies are, we find it gratifying that a simple analytical approach developed by physicists and mathematicians describes the actual wealth distributions of multiple nations with unprecedented precision and accuracy. Also rather curious is that these distributions display subtle but key features of complex physical systems. Most important, however, the fact that a sketch of the free market as simple and plausible as the affine wealth model gives rise to economies that are anything but free and fair should be both a cause for alarm and a call for action.

Referenced

"A Nonstandard Description of Wealth Concentration in Large-Scale Economies." Adrian Devitt-Lee et al. in *SIAM Journal on Applied Mathematics*, Vol. 78, No. 2, pages 996–1008; March 2018.

"The Affine Wealth Model: An Agent-Based Model of Asset Exchange That Allows for Negative-Wealth Agents and Its Empirical Validation." Jie Li et al. in *Physica A: Statistical Mechanics and Its Applications*, Vol. 516, pages 423–442; February 2019.

About the Author

Bruce M. Boghosian is a professor of mathematics at Tufts University, with research interests in applied dynamical systems and applied probability theory.

The Theory That Men Evolved to Hunt and Women Evolved to Gather Is Wrong

By Cara Ocobock & Sarah Lacy

Even if you're not an anthropologist, you've probably encountered one of this field's most influential notions, known as Man the Hunter. The theory proposes that hunting was a major driver of human evolution and that men carried this activity out to the exclusion of women. It holds that human ancestors had a division of labor, rooted in biological differences between males and females, in which males evolved to hunt and provide and females tended to children and domestic duties. It assumes that males are physically superior to females and that pregnancy and child-rearing reduce or eliminate a female's ability to hunt.

Man the Hunter has dominated the study of human evolution for nearly half a century and pervaded popular culture. It is represented in museum dioramas and textbook figures, Saturday morning cartoons and feature films. The thing is, it's wrong.

Mounting evidence from exercise science indicates that women are physiologically better suited than men to endurance efforts such as running marathons. This advantage bears on questions about hunting because a prominent hypothesis contends that early humans are thought to have pursued prey on foot over long distances until the animals were exhausted. Furthermore, the fossil and archaeological records, as well as ethnographic studies of modern-day hunter-gatherers, indicate that women have a long history of hunting game. We still have much to learn about female athletic performance and the lives of prehistoric women. Nevertheless, the data we do have signal that it is time to bury Man the Hunter for good.

The theory rose to prominence in 1968, when anthropologists Richard B. Lee and Irven DeVore published *Man the Hunter*, an edited collection of scholarly papers presented at a 1966 symposium on contemporary hunter-gatherer societies. The volume drew on ethnographic, archaeological and paleoanthropological evidence to argue that hunting is what drove human evolution and resulted in our suite of unique features. "Man's life as a hunter supplied all the other ingredients for achieving civilization: the genetic variability, the inventiveness, the systems of vocal communication, the coordination of social life," anthropologist William S. Laughlin writes in chapter 33 of the book. Because men were supposedly the ones hunting, proponents of the Man the Hunter theory assumed evolution was acting primarily on men, and women were merely passive beneficiaries of both the meat supply and evolutionary progress.

But *Man the Hunter*'s contributors often ignored evidence, sometimes in their own data, that countered their suppositions. For example, Hitoshi Watanabe focused on ethnographic data about the Ainu, an Indigenous population in northern Japan and its surrounding areas. Although Watanabe documented Ainu women hunting, often with the aid of dogs, he dismissed this finding in his interpretations and placed the focus squarely on men as the primary meat winners. He was superimposing the idea of male superiority through hunting onto the Ainu and into the past.

This fixation on male superiority was a sign of the times not just in academia but in society at large. In 1967, the year between the *Man the Hunter* conference and the publication of the edited volume, 20-year-old Kathrine Switzer entered the Boston Marathon under the name "K. V. Switzer," which obscured her gender. There were no official rules against women entering the race; it just was not done. When officials discovered that Switzer was a woman, race manager Jock Semple attempted to push her physically off the course.

At that time, the conventional wisdom was that women were incapable of completing such a physically demanding task and that attempting to do so could harm their precious reproductive capacities. Scholars following Man the Hunter dogma relied on this belief in women's limited physical capacities and the assumed burden of pregnancy and lactation to argue that only men hunted. Women had children to rear instead.

Today these biased assumptions persist in both the scientific literature and the public consciousness. Granted, women have recently been shown hunting in movies such as *Prey*, the newest installment of the popular Predator franchise, and on cable programs such as *Naked and Afraid* and *Women Who Hunt*. But social media trolls have viciously critiqued and labeled these depictions as part of a politically correct feminist agenda. They insist the creators of such works are trying to rewrite gender roles and evolutionary history in an attempt to co-opt "traditionally masculine" social spheres. Bystanders might be left wondering whether portrayals of women hunters are trying to make the past more inclusive than it really was—or whether Man the Hunter-style assumptions about the past are attempts to project sexism backward in time. Our recent surveys of the physiological and archaeological evidence for hunting capability and sexual division of labor in human evolution answer this question.

Before getting into the evidence, we need to first talk about sex and gender. "Sex" typically refers to biological sex, which can be defined by myriad characteristics such as chromosomes, hormone levels, gonads, external genitalia and secondary sex characteristics. The terms "female" and "male" are often used in relation to biological sex. "Gender" refers to how an individual identifies—woman, man, nonbinary, and so forth. Much of the scientific literature confuses and conflates female/male and woman/man terminology without providing definitions to clarify what it is referring to and why those terms were chosen. For the purpose of describing anatomical and physiological evidence, most of the literature uses "female" and "male," so we use those words here when discussing the results of such studies. For ethnographic and archaeological evidence, we are attempting to reconstruct social roles, for which the terms "woman" and "man" are usually used. Unfortunately, both these word sets assume a binary, which does not exist biologically, psychologically or socially. Sex and gender both exist as a spectrum, but it is difficult to add that nuance when citing the work of others.

It also bears mentioning that much of the research into exercise physiology, paleoanthropology, archaeology and ethnography has historically been conducted by men and focused on males. For example, Ella Smith of the Australian Catholic University and her colleagues found that in studies of nutrition and supplements, only 23 percent of participants were female. Emma Cowley, then at the University of North Carolina at Chapel Hill, and her colleagues found that among published studies focusing on athletic performance, only 6 percent had female-only participants; 31 percent looked exclusively at males. This massive disparity means we still know very little about female athletic performance, training and nutrition, leaving athletic trainers and coaches to treat females mostly as small males. It also means that much of the work we have to rely on to make our physiological arguments about female hunters in prehistory is based on research with small human sample sizes or rodent studies. We hope this state of affairs will inspire the next generation of scientists to ensure that females are represented in such studies. But even with the limited data available to us, we can show that Man the Hunter is a flawed theory and make the case that females in early human communities hunted, too.

From a biological standpoint, there are undeniable differences between females and males. When we discuss these differences, we are typically referring to means, averages of one group compared with another. Means obscure the vast range of variation in humans. For instance, although males tend to be larger and to have bigger hearts and lungs and more muscle mass, there are plenty of females who fall within the typical male range; the inverse is also true.

Overall, females are metabolically better suited for endurance activities, whereas males excel at short, powerful burst-type activities. You can think of it as marathoners (females) versus powerlifters (males). Much of this difference seems to be driven by the powers of the hormone estrogen.

Given the fitness world's persistent touting of the hormone testosterone for athletic success, you'd be forgiven for not knowing that estrogen, which females typically produce more of than males, plays an incredibly important role in athletic performance. It makes sense from an evolutionary standpoint, however. The estrogen receptor—the protein that estrogen binds to in order to do its work—is deeply ancient. Joseph Thornton of the University of Chicago and his colleagues have estimated that it is around 1.2 billion to 600 million years old—roughly twice as old as the testosterone receptor. In addition to helping regulate the reproductive system, estrogen influences fine-motor control and memory, enhances the growth and development of neurons, and helps to prevent hardening of the arteries.

Important for the purposes of this discussion, estrogen also improves fat metabolism. During exercise, estrogen seems to encourage the body to use stored fat for energy before stored carbohydrates. Fat contains more calories per gram than carbohydrates do, so it burns more slowly, which can delay fatigue during endurance activity. Not only does estrogen encourage fat burning, but it also promotes greater fat storage within muscles—marbling if you will—which makes that fat's energy more readily available. Adiponectin, another hormone that is typically present in higher amounts in females than in males, further enhances fat metabolism while sparing carbohydrates for future use, and it protects muscle from breakdown. Anne Friedlander of Stanford University and her colleagues found that females use as much as 70 percent more fat for energy during exercise than males.

Correspondingly, the muscle fibers of females differ from those of males. Females have more type I, or "slow-twitch," muscle fibers than males do. These fibers generate energy slowly by using fat. They are not all that powerful, but they take a long time to become fatigued. They are the endurance muscle fibers. Males, in contrast, typically have more type II ("fast-twitch") fibers, which use carbohydrates to provide quick energy and a great deal of power but tire rapidly.

Females also tend to have a greater number of estrogen receptors on their skeletal muscles compared with males. This arrangement makes these muscles more sensitive to estrogen, including to its protective effect after physical activity. Estrogen's ability to increase fat metabolism and regulate the body's response to the hormone insulin can help prevent muscle breakdown during intense exercise. Furthermore, estrogen appears to have a stabilizing effect on cell membranes that might otherwise rupture from acute stress brought on by heat and exercise. Ruptured cells release enzymes called creatine kinases, which can damage tissues.

Studies of females and males during and after exercise bolster these claims. Linda Lamont of the University of Rhode Island and her colleagues, as well as Michael Riddell of York University in Canada and his colleagues, found that females experienced less muscle breakdown than males after the same bouts of exercise. Tellingly, in a separate study, Mazen J. Hamadeh of York University and his colleagues found that males supplemented with estrogen suffered less muscle breakdown during cycling than those who didn't receive estrogen supplements. In a similar vein, research led by Ron Maughan of the University of St. Andrews in Scotland found that females were able to perform significantly more weight-lifting repetitions than males at the same percentages of their maximal strength.

If females are better able to use fat for sustained energy and keep their muscles in better condition during exercise, then they should be able to run greater distances with less fatigue relative to males. In fact, an analysis of marathons carried out by Robert Deaner of Grand Valley State University demonstrated that females tend to slow down less as a race progresses compared with males.

If you follow long-distance races, you might be thinking, wait—males are outperforming females in endurance events! But this is only sometimes the case. Females are more regularly dominating ultraendurance events such as the more than 260-mile Montane Spine foot race through England and Scotland, the 21-mile swim across the English Channel and the 4,300-mile Trans Am cycling race across the U.S. Sometimes female athletes compete in these races while attending to the needs of their children. In 2018 English runner Sophie Power ran the 105-mile Ultra-Trail du Mont-Blanc race in the Alps while still breastfeeding her three-month-old at rest stations.

Inequity between male and female athletes is a result not of inherent biological differences between the sexes but of biases in how they are treated in sports. As an example, some endurance-running events allow the use of professional runners called pacesetters to help competitors perform their best. Men are not permitted to act as pacesetters in many women's events because of the belief that they will make the women "artificially faster," as though women were not actually doing the running themselves.

The modern physiological evidence, along with historical examples, exposes deep flaws in the idea that physical inferiority prevented females from partaking in hunting during our evolutionary past. The evidence from prehistory further undermines this notion.

Consider the skeletal remains of ancient people. Differences in body size between females and males of a species, a phenomenon called sexual size dimorphism, correlate with social structure. In species with pronounced size dimorphism, larger males compete with one another for access to females, and among the great apes larger males socially dominate females. Low sexual size dimorphism is characteristic of egalitarian and monogamous species. Modern humans have low sexual size dimorphism compared with the other great apes. The same goes for human ancestors spanning the past two million years, suggesting that the social structure of humans changed from that of our chimpanzee-like ancestors.

Anthropologists also look at damage on our ancestors' skeletons for clues to their behavior. Neandertals are the best-studied extinct members of the human family because we have a rich fossil record of their remains. Neandertal females and males do not differ in their trauma patterns, nor do they exhibit sex differences in pathology from repetitive actions. Their skeletons show the same patterns of wear and tear. This finding suggests that they were doing the same things, from ambush-hunting large game animals to processing hides for leather. Yes, Neandertal women were spearing woolly rhinoceroses, and Neandertal men were making clothing.

Males living in the Upper Paleolithic—the cultural period between roughly 45,000 and 10,000 years ago, when early modern humans entered Europe—do show higher rates of a set of injuries to the right elbow region known as thrower's elbow, which could mean they were more likely than females to throw spears. But it does not mean women were not hunting, because this period is also when people invented the bow and arrow, hunting nets and fishing hooks. These more sophisticated tools enabled humans to catch a wider variety of animals; they were also easier on hunters' bodies. Women may have favored hunting tactics that took advantage of these new technologies.

What is more, females and males were buried in the same way in the Upper Paleolithic. Their bodies were interred with the same kinds of artifacts, or grave goods, suggesting that the groups they lived in did not have social hierarchies based on sex.

Ancient DNA provides additional clues about social structure and potential gender roles in ancestral human communities. Patterns of variation in the Y chromosome, which is paternally inherited, and in mitochondrial DNA, which is maternally inherited, can reveal differences in how males and females dispersed after reaching maturity. Thanks to analyses of DNA extracted from fossils, we now know of three Neandertal groups that engaged in patrilocality—wherein males were more likely to stay in the group they were born into and females moved to other groups—although we do not know how widespread this practice was.

Patrilocality is believed to have been an attempt to avoid incest by trading potential mates with other groups. Nevertheless, many Neandertals show both genetic and anatomical evidence of repeated inbreeding in their ancestry. They lived in small, nomadic groups with low population densities and endured frequent local extinctions, which produced much lower levels of genetic diversity than we see in living humans. This is probably why we don't see any evidence in their skeletons of sex-based differences in behavior.

For those practicing a foraging subsistence strategy in small family groups, flexibility and adaptability are much more important than rigid roles, gendered or otherwise. Individuals get injured or die, and the availability of animal and plant foods changes with the seasons. All group members need to be able to step into any role depending on the situation, whether that role is hunter or breeding partner.

Observations of recent and contemporary foraging societies provide direct evidence of women participating in hunting. The most cited examples come from the Agta people of the Philippines. Agta women hunt while menstruating, pregnant and breastfeeding, and they have the same hunting success as Agta men.

They are hardly alone. A recent study of ethnographic data spanning the past 100 years—much of which was ignored by Man the Hunter contributors—found that women from a wide range of cultures hunt animals for food. Abigail Anderson and Cara Wall-Scheffler, both then at Seattle Pacific University, and their colleagues reported that 79 percent of the 63 foraging societies with clear descriptions of their hunting strategies feature women hunters. The women participate in hunting regardless of their childbearing status. These findings directly challenge the Man the Hunter assumption that women's bodies and childcare responsibilities limit their efforts to gathering foods that cannot run away.

So much about female exercise physiology and the lives of prehistoric women remains to be discovered. But the idea that in the past men were hunters and women were not is absolutely unsupported by the limited evidence we have. Female physiology is optimized for exactly the kinds of endurance activities involved in procuring game animals for food. And ancient women and men appear to have engaged in the same foraging activities rather than upholding a sex-based division of labor. It was the arrival some 10,000 years ago of agriculture, with its intensive investment in land, population growth and resultant clumped resources, that led to rigid gendered roles and economic inequality.

Now when you think of "cave people," we hope, you will imagine a mixed-sex group of hunters encircling an errant reindeer or knapping stone tools together rather than a heavy-browed man with a club over one shoulder and a trailing bride. Hunting may have been remade as a masculine activity in recent times, but for most of human history, it belonged to everyone.

About the Authors

Cara Ocobock studies human biology at the University of Notre Dame. A former powerlifter, she explores the physiological and behavioral mechanisms necessary to cope with and adapt to extreme climates and high levels of physical activity.

Sarah Lacy is a biological anthropologist at the University of Delaware. She studies the oral and respiratory health differences between Neandertals and early modern humans. Lacy is also a trained doula and an advocate for safer pregnancy and birth in the U.S.

Section 5: Earth's Strangest Places

5.1   Volcanic Activity, Not Giant Bears, Created Enigmatic Devils Tower
      By Scott K. Johnson

5.2   Ocean Discoveries Are Revising Long-Held Truths about Life
      By Timothy Shank

5.3   'Dark Oxygen' Discovered Coming from Mineral Deposits on Deep Seafloor
      By Allison Parshall

5.4   One Mystery of Stonehenge's Origins Has Finally Been Solved
      By Scott Hershberger

5.5   King Tut Mysteries Endure 100 Years after Discovery
      By Zach Zorich

Volcanic Activity, Not Giant Bears, Created Enigmatic Devils Tower

By Scott K. Johnson

Devils Tower in Wyoming is such an extraordinary sight that its creation myth almost seems possible. Giant bears are said to have scratched its surface attempting to climb to the top. But the vertical lines adorning the sides of the almost 390-meter-tall rock are not claw marks. They are actually the edges of roughly hexagonal columns of igneous rock, similar to other geometric landmarks such as Ireland's Giant's Causeway or Devils Postpile in California. The columns form as molten rock cools and contracts, cracking apart. But how did the sky-scraping columns of Devils Tower form—belowground or as part of a violent eruption?

A number of hypotheses for the 49-million-year-old monolith have been put forward over the years but most involve a subterranean explanation. The most popular explanations today are that it was either born as an inflating half dome of magma squeezed in between subsurface layers of rock or within a conduit deep inside a volcano.

Prokop Závada, a geologist at The Czech Academy of Sciences, and three of his colleagues came to this mystery by way of a stout butte known as Bořeň in the Czech Republic that shares some similarities with Devils Tower (although it is more rounded and covered with trees). The researchers concluded that Bořeň is the product of a sudden type of volcano called a maar-diatreme, which blasts a crater in the land surface when a body of magma underground encounters groundwater. After the blast, they believe, a flat dome of lava filled the crater. Erosion ate away at the edges of that dome until only the innermost portion remained, standing as an isolated butte. Given its similarities to Bořeň, Závada and his team turned their attention to Devils Tower to see if the same explanation would fit there.

There were two primary characteristics the researchers used to hone in on the origins of Devils Tower: the shape of its distinctive columns and the alignment of magnetic minerals within them. The researchers were permitted by the National Park Service to collect one new rock sample to analyze its magnetic properties, and added this to existing measurements made over 30 years ago from a few other sections of the tower. Near the base the tiny, needle-shaped magnetic minerals within the rock are generally close to vertical, the result of the direction the magma flowed before it solidified. Closer to the top of the formation, however, the orientation of those minerals becomes horizontal.

With that information in hand, the researchers turned to models, both digital and physical: The physical one involved squeezing soft plaster upward through an inverted cone full of sediment until it formed a mound atop the surface. This approximated the eruption of lava following the explosive phase of a maar-diatreme volcano. When the plaster hardened, the researchers could cut it open to examine the interior structure, highlighted by some colorant that formed stripes distorted by flow. Because they mixed in some magnetic particles as well, they could also measure their orientation just as they had done at Devils Tower. The digital model was a computer simulation of cooling igneous rock. It allowed the researchers to compare columns that would be produced in different scenarios of the tower's formation. Columns form perpendicular to the surface along which the rock cools, so they can tell you about the original shape of the body of molten rock.

The vertical columns of Devils Tower, which splay outward near the bottom, match the pattern expected if the formation were indeed the plug in the neck of a funnel-shaped crater filled with a dome of erupted lava. In that portion of the plaster models the orientation of the magnetic particles also matches the orientation of the minerals from Devils Tower: closer to vertical around the base and horizontal near the top. In a paper published in *Geosphere* Závada and his team thus concluded that like Bořeň in the Czech Republic, "Devils Tower is a remnant of a coulee or low lava dome that was emplaced into a broad phreatomagmatic crater at the top of a maar-diatreme volcano."

Western Washington University's Bernard Housen, who was not involved in the study, finds the work "interesting and certainly very plausible" but he is not convinced it rules out the other possibilities. There just isn't very much data from Devils Tower itself, given that so little geologic sampling of the national monument has been allowed. "So, it is likely that the origin of Devils Tower will remain uncertain in part due to the protections we have enabled to make sure it is preserved," Housen says.

It might be possible to study the similar, if less spectacular, buttes in the vicinity of Devils Tower, however, which likely formed in the same way—with or without the help of giant bears.

About the Author

Scott K. Johnson is a hydrogeologist by day, Earth science instructor at Madison College by the other part of the day, and freelance science writer for Ars Technica by night.

Ocean Discoveries Are Revising Long-Held Truths about Life

By Timothy Shank

For more than 50 years deep-sea exploration has been a continuous fount of discoveries that change how we think about life in the ocean, on dry land and even beyond our planet. Consider the following three events.

On October 16, 1968, a cable tethering the submersible *Alvin* to a research ship located 100 miles off Nantucket broke. The sub sank to the seafloor more than 5,000 feet below; the crew of three escaped safely. Nearly a year later, when a team brought *Alvin* back to the surface, the biggest surprise was that the crew's lunch—bologna sandwiches and apples in a plastic box—was strikingly well preserved. Bacteriological and biochemical assays proved it. Someone even took a bite. Subsequent experiments in the Woods Hole Oceanographic Institution laboratory where I'm writing this article found that rates of microbial degradation in the retrieved samples were 10 to 100 times slower than expected. This discovery, and others, led to the conclusion that metabolic and growth rates among deep-sea organisms were much slower than those of comparable species at the ocean's surface.

In 1977 scientists diving in the restored *Alvin* made another historic discovery—the first in-person observations of life around hot, hydrothermal vents rising from the seafloor. This sighting overturned the long-held view that our entire planetary food web was built on photosynthesis—using sunlight's energy to convert carbon dioxide and water into complex carbohydrates and oxygen. The hydrothermal organisms, and the entire ecosystem, thrived in pure darkness, converting chemicals in the vent fluid into life-sustaining compounds through a process we now call chemosynthesis.

If that revelation wasn't surprising enough, an expedition I was part of in 1993 exposed an earlier mistaken belief. We had discovered a significant hydrothermal vent ecosystem on the East Pacific Rise. The system had been destroyed by a seafloor eruption just a few years earlier, yet it had already been bountifully recolonized. A bologna sandwich might decay so slowly in the deep that you could eat it a year later, but it turned out that biological processes in the deep sea could be extremely fast as well.

Each new ocean discovery that disrupts old dogma reinforces a much larger truth: the ocean is far more complex—and much more intertwined with our own lives—than we ever imagined. For much of the 20th century, for example, scientists maintained that the deep ocean was a harsh, monotonous place of perpetual darkness, frigid temperatures, limited food and extreme pressure—conditions that should make complex forms of life impossible. But new tools for observing, sensing and sampling the deep ocean, such as increasingly sophisticated underwater vehicles with high-definition camera systems, have demonstrated that biodiversity in the darkest depths may rival that of rain forests and tropical coral reefs. These missions have further revealed that the depths are far from uniform; like kangaroo habitat in Australia and tiger lands in Asia, they are home to evolutionarily distinct biogeographic regions.

We are beginning to appreciate how connected these realms are to our own. The rapid three-dimensional change of conditions such as temperature, salinity and oxygen concentration in the deep ocean and the currents and eddies that establish the boundaries of these provinces are expected to fundamentally change as the effects of human activity reach ever farther below the surface. Already lobsters are moving to deeper, colder waters and molting at different times of the year. Commercially important groundfish such as cod and haddock are migrating poleward in search of more suitable habitat.

We are seeing that the ocean's biogeographic boundaries are neither immutable nor beyond the imprint of humans. In studies, more than half of sampled hadal organisms—those living in the deepest parts of the ocean, beyond 20,000 feet—had plastics in their gut. PCBs, which were banned in the U.S. in 1979 and phased out internationally as part of the Stockholm Convention beginning in 2001, are also common in tissues of animals from the extreme bottoms of the sea.

We are also starting to learn that life in the deep might have things to teach us. Deep-sea fish produce biomolecules called osmolytes that permit cellular functions, such as the precise folding and unfolding of proteins, to proceed unimpeded by crushing water-column pressures exceeding 15,000 pounds per square inch. Medical researchers have determined that some of these molecules could help treat Alzheimer's disease, which is characterized by misfolded proteins. In addition, decoding the genes that govern traits we see in deep-sea animals, such as those that stave off errors in DNA replication, transcription and translation, might be used in therapies for cancer and other afflictions.

The greatest paradigm that ocean exploration may tear down is that Earth represents the sole example of life in the universe. Life might have existed on Mars when it hosted liquid water, and the fact that Earth and Mars have shared ejected material in the past means we could have exchanged the building blocks of life. But the discovery of chemosynthetic life on Earth and the more recent finding of perhaps 13 liquid-water oceans underneath the icy shells of moons such as Jupiter's Europa and Saturn's Enceladus—places that may have been too distant to have shared life-bearing material with Earth in the past—raise the possibility of a second, independent genesis of life. And if life can form twice in one solar system, then it could be anywhere we look in the heavens.

About the Author

Timothy Shank is a biologist, director of the Molecular Ecology and Evolution Lab at Woods Hole Oceanographic Institution, and co-leader of the Deep-Ocean Genomes Project.

'Dark Oxygen' Discovered Coming from Mineral Deposits on Deep Seafloor

By Allison Parshall

The flat, pitch-black seabed of the Pacific Ocean's Clarion-Clipperton Zone (CCZ) is littered with what looks like hunks of charcoal. These unassuming mineral deposits, called polymetallic nodules, host a unique deep-sea ecosystem, much of which scientists have yet to catalog. And the deposits are also a key target for companies that are looking to mine the deep sea because they contain metals, such as manganese and cobalt, that are used to make batteries.

Now researchers have discovered that these valuable nodules do something remarkable: they produce oxygen and do so without sunlight. "This is a totally new and unexpected finding," says Lisa Levin, an emeritus professor of biological oceanography at the Scripps Institution of Oceanography, who was not involved in the research.

According to Boston University microbiologist Jeffrey Marlow, the idea that some of Earth's oxygen gas may come not from photosynthesizing organisms but from inanimate minerals in total darkness "really strongly goes against what we traditionally think of as where oxygen is made and how it's made." Marlow is a co-author of the new study, which was published in *Nature Geoscience*.

The story of discovery goes back to 2013, when deep-sea ecologist Andrew Sweetman was facing a frustrating problem. He was part of a research team that had been trying to measure how much oxygen organisms on the CCZ seafloor consumed. The researchers sent landers down more than 13,000 feet to create enclosed chambers on the seabed that would track how oxygen levels in the water fell over time.

But oxygen levels did not fall. Instead they rose significantly. Thinking the sensors were broken, Sweetman sent the instruments back to the manufacturer to be recalibrated. "This happened four or five times" over the course of five years, says Sweetman, who studies seafloor ecology and biogeochemistry at the Scottish Association for Marine Science. "I literally told my students, 'Throw the sensors in the bin. They just do not work.'"

Then, in 2021, he was able to go back to the CCZ on an environmental survey expedition sponsored by a deep-sea mining firm called the Metals Company. Again, his team used deep-sea landers to make enclosed chambers on the seafloor. The chambers enclosed encased sediment, nodules, living organisms and seawater and monitored oxygen levels. Sweetman and his team used a different technique to measure oxygen this time, but they observed the same strange results: oxygen levels increased dramatically. "Suddenly, I realized that I'd been ignoring this hugely significant process, and I just kicked myself," Sweetman says.

"My first thought was microbiology, and that's because I'm a microbiologist," Marlow says. It wasn't a far-fetched idea: scientists had recently uncovered some ways that microbes such as bacteria and archaea could generate "dark oxygen" in the absence of sunlight. In lab tests that reproduced conditions on the seafloor in the new study, the researchers poisoned the seawater with mercury chloride to kill off microbes. Yet the oxygen levels still increased.

If this dark oxygen didn't come from a biological process, then it must have come from a geological one, the researchers reasoned. They tested and ruled out a few possible hypotheses—such as that radioactivity in the nodules was separating oxygen out of the seawater or that some other environmental factor was separating oxygen gas out of the manganese oxide in the nodules.

Then, one day in 2022, Sweetman was watching a video about deep-sea mining when he heard the nodules referred to as "a battery in a rock"—a phrase favored by Gerard Barron, the Metals Company's CEO. That led Sweetman to wonder, "The metals that are in these nodules, could they somehow be acting as natural geobatteries?" If so, they could potentially split seawater into hydrogen and oxygen through a process called seawater electrolysis. (You may have done this in chemistry class by running a battery's electric current through salt water, causing hydrogen and oxygen gas to bobble up.)

"Batteries in a rock" was just a metaphor, as far as the scientists knew—the fact that the nodules contain metals used to make batteries does not mean that they are electrically charged themselves. To create a charge, positive and negative ions would have to be separated to some degree within a nodule, creating a difference in electrical potential. To see whether that was occurring, Sweetman flew to Illinois to test the nodules' electric charge with Franz Geiger, a physical chemist at Northwestern University.

"Amazingly, there was almost a volt on the surface of these nodules," Sweetman says—for comparison, a AA battery carries about 1.5 volts. The researchers' leading theory is that this charge is splitting seawater to create oxygen, though they have not yet tested whether disabling the nodules' electric charge halts oxygen production. The scientists plan to test this in future studies.

Geiger theorizes that the polymetallic nodules become charged as they grow, with different metals depositing irregularly over time. Nodules form around a small object, such as a shark's tooth. If you cut one open, "they look like cross sections of tree rings" or like layers of an onion, Geiger says. These metal layers grow only millimeters every million years, and the types of metals being deposited change over time, potentially creating a gradient in charge between each layer that results in electrical potential. That doesn't explain why there are differences in charge on the surfaces of the nodules, but Geiger theorizes that the nodules are porous enough to leave some of their inner layers exposed.

Rocks are not known to carry charge like this, Geiger says. This "is one of the most fascinating things [I and my lab] have ever worked on," he adds.

It still isn't clear whether (or to what extent) these nodules create oxygen naturally on the seabed. In most experiments, oxygen concentrations in the chambers plateaued after two days. That might indicate that the lander changed something about the environment—for example, by kicking up sediment—which then instigated the oxygen production. It's also possible that oxygen production eventually stopped because of a "bottle effect" within the enclosed chamber, Marlow says. "The products build up, the reactants go away, and then the reaction sort of stops. But in an open system... It could be a more consistent process," he explains.

Bo Barker Jørgensen, a marine biogeochemist at the Max Planck Institute for Marine Microbiology in Bremen, Germany, says the findings are "very odd" and raise many questions. (Jørgensen was not involved in the research but was one of the paper's peer reviewers for *Nature Geoscience*.) He is skeptical that these nodules produce oxygen when they are left undisturbed on the seabed. Still, he adds, "it seems to be some electrolytic reaction on the manganese nodule surface that does indeed produce oxygen. And that in itself is a very interesting observation that has not been observed before, to my knowledge."

The researchers still have no idea what role this nodule-produced oxygen may play in the seabed ecosystems of the CCZ. Environmental surveys have shown that the nodules and surrounding sediment are a habitat for deep-sea life: everything from single-celled microbes to "megafauna," animals that can be seen with the naked eye, such as fish, sea stars and worms. Approximately half of the megafauna cataloged during the 2013 environmental survey were found only on the nodules.

Like most of the deep ocean, the seafloor of the CCZ is a "poorly understood ecosystem," Levin says. "We haven't even discovered most of the species in the deep sea, let alone studied them."

Deep-sea mining projects proposed across the CCZ would extract nodules from swaths of the seafloor. The International Seabed Authority (ISA), which governs the seafloor in international waters, is currently discussing rules and regulations for mining the nodules and other deep-sea targets. Twenty-seven nations, including 26 member states of the ISA, have called for a moratorium, precautionary pause or ban on deep-sea mining.

"I don't think [this research is] a 'nail in the coffin' for deep-sea mining—that has never been the intention," Sweetman says. "It's just another thing that we now need to take into account when it comes to deciding, 'Do we go and mine the deep ocean, or don't we?' To me, that decision needs to be based on sound scientific advice and input."

About the Author

Allison Parshall is an associate news editor at Scientific American *who often covers biology, health, technology and physics. She edits the magazine's Contributors column and has previously edited the Advances section. As a multimedia journalist, Parshall contributes to* Scientific American's *podcast Science Quickly. Her work includes a three-part miniseries on music-making artificial intelligence. Her work has also appeared in* Quanta Magazine *and* Inverse. *Parshall graduated from New York University's Arthur L. Carter Journalism Institute with a master's degree in science, health and environmental reporting. She has a bachelor's degree in psychology from Georgetown University. Follow Parshall on X (formerly Twitter) @parshallison.*

One Mystery of Stonehenge's Origins Has Finally Been Solved

By Scott Hershberger

For more than four centuries, archaeologists and geologists have sought to determine the geographical origins of the stones used to build Stonehenge thousands of years ago. Pinning down the source of the large blocks known as sarsens that form the bulk of the monument has proved especially elusive. Now researchers have resolved the mystery: 50 of the 52 extant sarsens at Stonehenge came from the West Woods site in the English county of Wiltshire, located 25 kilometers to the north of Stonehenge. The findings were published on Wednesday in *Science Advances*.

Geologists can often use macroscopic and microscopic features of rocks to match them to the outcropping from which they were taken. Such techniques have allowed researchers to determine that many of Stonehenge's smaller "bluestones" were brought from southwestern Wales. But "the trouble with sarsen stone is that it's all the same," says study co-author Katy Whitaker, a graduate student at the University of Reading in England and an assistant listing adviser at Historic England. "When you look at it under the microscope, you see quartz sand grains stuck together with more quartz." So the team turned to x-ray fluorescence spectrometry, a nondestructive technique that bombards a sample with x-rays and analyzes the wavelengths of light that sample emits in response, which can show its chemical makeup. The technique revealed the presence of trace elements, or those found in minute quantities, on the surface of Stonehenge's sarsens. Almost all of those stones shared a remarkably similar chemical composition, indicating that they originated together. The data were insufficient to pinpoint where that source was, however.

The team's breakthrough came unexpectedly in 2018, when a sample core that had been drilled from one of Stonehenge's sarsens during a 1958 restoration project was returned to England after it spent 60 years in a private collection. The researchers were granted permission to destroy part of the core for a more detailed analysis. "We quietly jumped up and down with excitement," says lead author David Nash, a physical geographer at the University of Brighton in England. Using two types of mass spectrometry, the team determined the levels of 22 trace elements in the core and compared them with the levels in sarsen samples from 20 different sites dotting southern England. The chemical signature of the core exactly matched that of one of the sites—West Woods, which encompasses about six square kilometers.

The finding "looks to be fairly convincing and fairly conclusive," says Joshua Pollard, an archaeologist at the University of Southampton in England, who was not involved in the new research. "It's a major achievement." Located just south of the River Kennet, West Woods has often been overlooked in archaeological research, he adds. Until now the prevailing speculation had posited that the sarsens originated to the north of the river, in the Marlborough Downs.

Although Nash's team identified the origin of 50 sarsens, the last two—Stone 26 and Stone 160—did not match any of the sites studied, nor did they match each other. Because up to 30 more sarsens have been lost since the construction of Stonehenge, it is impossible to know if Stones 26 and 160 are unique or the remnants of a large group of the rocks brought from outside West Woods.

For Nash, the most intriguing implication of the finding is that the stones from West Woods were likely all moved during the monument's second phase of construction, around 2500 B.C. "What it really brings home for me is the Herculean effort that went into making this structure in a reasonably short time window," he says. How Neolithic people managed to transport the massive stones—which have an average weight of 20 metric tons—remains unknown. But archaeologists agree that large-scale social coordination was necessary.

Future research will seek to uncover the route that the builders of Stonehenge used to transport the stones. And the geochemical techniques pioneered by Nash's team could yield insights at other prehistoric henge monuments in England. "There are endless questions, endless areas that need further investigation and thought," Pollard says. "This is a journey that's not going to end."

About the Author

Scott Hershberger was a 2020 AAAS Mass Media Fellow at Scientific American.

King Tut Mysteries Endure 100 Years after Discovery

By Zach Zorich

It is one of the most iconic discoveries in all of archaeology—the treasure-filled tomb of the young Egyptian pharaoh Tutankhamun, better known as King Tut. One hundred years ago today British archaeologist Howard Carter and an Egyptian excavation team found the boy king's final resting place. Scholars have been studying the royal tomb and its owner ever since. From this work the broad outlines of the life and times of Tut have emerged. Many mysteries remain, however, including how the young pharaoh was related to Queen Nefertiti (herself a subject of debate), how influential he was as a ruler and how he died. Now new findings are emerging that could fill in some of the missing details. But as ever, debates rage over how to interpret them.

The key to Tut's discovery was dogged perseverance. By November 4, 1922, Carter and his team had spent five futile years searching for an undiscovered royal tomb in Egypt's Valley of the Kings. The prevailing wisdom said that everything the valley had to offer had already been found. Carter decided to spend what was to be his final field season digging beneath a group of huts that housed the ancient tomb builders. "We had almost made up our minds that we were beaten . . . ," he and archaeologist Arthur Cruttenden Mace wrote in *The Discovery of the Tomb of Tutankhamen*, their account of the expedition. "Hardly had we set hoe to ground in our last despairing effort than we made a discovery beyond our wildest dreams."

Beneath those huts, the excavation team uncovered a step cut into the rock. The next day the team dug out a steep staircase and a door sealed with plaster and stamped with the royal necropolis seal. Carter waited to open the door until his benefactor George Edward Stanhope Molyneux Herbert, fifth earl of Carnarvon, who had funded his work in the valley for all those years, could travel to the site. On November 24, 1922, it was cleared to reveal a corridor, followed by a 30-foot-long passageway that ended in another door. On November 26, 1922, Carter broke open a small hole in the door and stuck a candle through, casting the first light into the chamber in nearly 3,300 years. The sight held him speechless as his eyes adjusted. "Details of the room emerged slowly from the mist, strange animals, statues, and gold—everywhere the glint of gold," Carter wrote in *The Discovery of the Tomb of Tutankhamen*. He was looking into the antechamber of the tomb of Tutankhamun, a ruler who sat on his throne for only around 10 years but did so at a pivotal time in Egyptian history.

Carter went on to carry out a meticulous, decade-long study of the four chambers that make up the tomb and more than 5,000 artifacts within them. "I'm grateful that it was he who found that tomb," says Egyptologist Salima Ikram of the American University in Cairo. "Had it been any number of other individuals, we would have had much less left to us." Although Carter complicated his legacy by taking artifacts from the tomb for his personal collection, he was considerably more careful in his documentation of the tomb than a number of other excavators working in Egypt at the time. Carter enlisted archaeological photographer Harry Burton, who was working with an expedition sponsored by the Metropolitan Museum of Art in New York City, to photograph the excavation of the tomb, documenting each chamber in detail before any objects were moved. Each artifact was given a number and drawn on a map. Carter "was trained under the most important archaeologist of that time, Sir Flinders Petrie," says Zahi Hawass, former head of Egypt's Ministry of Antiquities. "Petrie changes this man from a draftsman, whose drafts were not great, to one of the most important excavators at that time." Carter's methods are still used by modern Egyptologists to document tombs or other rooms full of artifacts, albeit with updated technology.

Through the work of Carter and his successors, a picture of Tut and his family began to coalesce. Tutankhamun was the son of

Section 5: Earth's Strangest Places

Pharaoh Akhenaten, who renounced the sun god Amun, the deity with the most economically and politically powerful religious cult. Egyptians had worshipped Amun as their chief god for hundreds of years. Akhenaten replaced him by elevating a sun god called Aten, who was previously only a minor religious figure. Before his father's death in 1336 B.C.E., Tutankhamun was named "Tutankh*aten*," which means "the living image of Aten." Akhenaten showed his devotion to Aten by moving Egypt's capital from Thebes to a new city he had built on an uninhabited piece of land near the Nile. The city had a massive temple dedicated to his new god, and he called it Akhetaten (today it is known as Amarna).

The temples of Egyptian gods served as centers of trade and places where food and wealth could be distributed to local populations. Without the powerful cult of Amun carrying out this business, Akhenaten's kingdom was thrown into turmoil. The cult of Aten did not seem to serve the public very well. Remains of the people who lived at Akhetaten show that much of the population was malnourished and endured lives of heavy manual labor, probably building Akhenaten's city.

Tutankhamun's story is intertwined with that of Akhenaten's principal wife Nefertiti, who was often depicted as equal in power to her husband. Her role as co-ruler of Egypt has made her a subject of fascination for scholars. How her time as a ruler ended and the transition to Tutankhamun's reign occurred are both part of the story of how Egypt was changing as the cult of Aten ended. She was probably not Tutankhamun's mother—one of Akhenaten's secondary wives, Kiya, is thought to have given birth to him. Artwork from Amarna that depicts the royal family often shows Nefertiti with her daughters but not a son.

After Akhenaten's death, an enigmatic pharaoh named Smenkhkara took the throne. This ruler's identity is a matter of intense debate. Some Egyptologists speculate that Smenkhkara may have been Nefertiti using a different name, which would make her one of the very few women to rule Egypt alone. "I think that it's possible that Nefertiti was ruling as a king," Ikram says. "Even in

Akhenaten's time, so much of her iconography was that of a male king, smiting enemies and doing things like that."

A pottery shard bearing Smenkhkara's name, found by Hawass's team at a city called the "Dazzling Aten" near the Valley of the Kings, supports this view. "This is a really big discovery because we don't know who Smenkhkara is," Hawass says. "I believe now Smenkhkara could be Nefertiti." A figurine showing a female ruler that was found in Tut's tomb bolsters Hawass's belief. It was not unusual for a ruler to change their name following a big political change during their reign, he says. Another female ruler, Hatshepsut, also changed her name to take on a male persona as pharaoh more than 100 years before Nefertiti, Hawass says.

The idea that Smenkhkara was Nefertiti using a different name has its skeptics, however. Joyce Tyldesley, a professor of Egyptology at the University of Manchester in England believes that Smenkhkara was a brother or half-brother of Tutankhamun. Barry Kemp, a professor emeritus of Egyptology at the University of Cambridge and director of excavations at Amarna, notes that a drawing in the tomb of Meryra II, a senior scribe and administrator, depicts the royal line of succession. "The king is labeled Ankh-kheperura Smenkhkara and the queen as Meretaten, Akhenaten's eldest daughter [by Nefertiti]," Kemp explains, "I find it perverse to argue that the former is Nefertiti."

Smenkhkara only ruled for about four years. Then, in 1332 B.C.E., Tutankhamun ascended the throne at the age of eight or nine to preside over a nation in upheaval. Egyptologists have speculated that he was a puppet king whose strings were being pulled by older men who had served as his father's advisers: Ay, who would become Tutankhamun's successor as pharaoh, and Horemheb, general of Egypt's army and the man who would succeed Ay a few years later. Early in his reign Tut renounced the worship of Aten and reinstated the worship of Amun. He also moved the capital from Amarna back to the city of Thebes. Tyldesley observes that Tut was very young when these events transpired, making it unlikely that the changes were his idea.

Section 5: Earth's Strangest Places

New evidence about Akhenaten's religious revolution and Tutankhamun's counterrevolution is also emerging from Hawass's excavations at the Dazzling Aten. After less than two years of work at the site, Hawass's team has uncovered much of the main street that divided the city into eastern and western parts. The street is bordered by curved mud-brick walls that were parts of buildings that housed workshops that were used during Tutankhamun's reign for making jewelry, leather sandals, clothing, amulets, statues and mud bricks. The team has also found an artificial lake that served as the city's water source. Intriguingly, drawings on the walls dating to the time of Akhenaten's father, Pharaoh Amenhotep III, depict the Aten exactly as he was shown at Amarna. Amenhotep III also refers to himself and his palace at Malqata as "Dazzling Aten." Hawass believes that the worship of Aten was fully formed even before the reign of Akhenaten. "For the first time, we can confirm that the idea of Aten was not from Akhenaten as everyone believes," he says. "Aten was created by Amenhotep III."

Fresh insights into the life of Tutankhamun may come from DNA analyses. Previous studies of ancient DNA obtained from Tut and several other members of the royal family revealed clues to his incestuous lineage. Now Hawass is involved with a DNA study of two unidentified mummies found in the Valley of the Kings. He believes they may be Nefertiti and Queen Ankhesenamun, the wife of Tutankhamun. Hawass expects the results of the DNA analysis in December. If the mummies do belong to members of Tutankhamun's family, the work could resolve some questions about how he was related to Nefertiti and other members of his dynasty.

The DNA evidence may not settle the matter, though. The generations of inbreeding that occurred among Egyptian royalty limit the conclusions that can be drawn from genetic studies, Ikram says. It may be hard to discern a sister from a close cousin when a family shares so much DNA in common.

Despite 100 years of study and technological progress, many questions about Tutankhamun remain—including the cause of his early death between the ages of 17 and 20. Researchers have proposed all manner of imaginative hypotheses for his demise, ranging from murder to a chariot accident to a hippopotamus attack. According to Ikram, CT scans of Tut's mummy have failed to provide a definitive answer. However he died, the most important legacy of Tutankhamun's brief reign may not have anything to do with restoring the cults of the old gods to Egypt. He is also great at drawing tourists to the nation. "Tutankhamun, I swear to God, is the best Egyptian pharaoh because he's the one who has been making Egypt's economy boom, or at least break even, ever since 1922," Ikram says. "Show me another king who's done that!"

About the Author

Zach Zorich is a freelance writer and a contributing editor at Archaeology Magazine.

GLOSSARY

advent Arrival or invention.

altruism Actions that benefit another, rather than oneself.

base A class of chemicals characterized by spare electrons, which reacts with acids. DNA is comprised of four bases.

benign Of no known negative impact.

decipher To interpret or decode.

disequilibrium Organized in a way that is out of physical or chemical balance.

egalitarian Characterized by equal distribution of power or resources.

elusive Difficult to locate.

epiphany Sudden realization or insight.

genome Sequence of genetic information in a particular individual in a species.

heretical A manner of acting that is contrary to established belief.

hominid A family of primates that includes humans, proto-human ancestors, and some great apes.

imperceptible Impossible to see or detect.

metabolism The chemical processes that maintain a living organism.

oscillating Regularly rotating, waving, or pulsing.

plausibility Likelihood or possibility.

predisposition A tendency toward, as in a disease.

rear-guard A term of military origin that describes the last of a group to change their beliefs.

sleight of hand A magic trick or, metaphorically, an act of deception or oversimplification.

Standard Model The current, most complete set of physical descriptions of the known elemental forces and particles.

ubiquitous Widespread or abundant.

FURTHER INFORMATION

"The Allure of Mysteries." The British Psychological Society, https://www.bps.org.uk/psychologist/allure-mysteries.

"Mysteries of the Universe." National Aeronautics and Space Administration (NASA), https://www.nasa.gov/specials/60counting/universe.html.

Bouzid, Samia, Katie Hafner, and the Lost Women of Science Initiative. "Elizabeth Bates and the Search for the Roots of Human Language." *Scientific American*, April 25, 2024, https://www.scientificamerican.com/article/elizabeth-bates-and-the-search-for-the-roots-of-human-language/.

Dev, Sukhenda B. "Unsolved Problems in Biology—The State of Current Thinking." *Progress in Biophysics and Molecular Biology*, March 2015, https://www.sciencedirect.com/science/article/pii/S0079610715000115?via%3Dihub.

Elliot, Natalie. "Life Is Complicated—Literally, Astrobiologists Say." *Scientific American*, November 23, 2021, https://www.scientificamerican.com/article/life-is-complicated-literally-astrobiologists-say/.

Fortenberry, Ryan C. "The First Molecule in the Universe." *Scientific American*, February 1, 2020, https://www.scientificamerican.com/article/the-first-molecule-in-the-universe/.

Goff, Philip. "Why the Mystery of Consciousness Is Deeper Than We Thought." *Scientific American*, July 3, 2024, https://www.scientificamerican.com/article/the-mystery-of-consciousness-is-deeper-than-we-thought/.

Koch, Christof. "Is Death Reversible?" *Scientific American*, October 1, 2019, https://www.scientificamerican.com/article/is-death-reversible/.

CITATIONS

1.1 The First Gene on Earth May Have Been a Hybrid by Andy Extance (June 22, 2020); 1.2 The Future of Man—How Will Evolution Change Humans? by Peter Ward (January 1, 2009); 1.3 Evidence Implies That Animals Feel Empathy by Frans B. M. de Waal (September 1, 2015); 1.4 The Search for Extraterrestrial Life as We Don't Know It by Sarah Scoles (February 1, 2023); 2.1 The Weirdest Particles in the Universe by Clara Moskowitz (June 7, 2023); 2.2 Why Aren't We Made of Antimatter? by Luke Caldwell (February 1, 2024); 2.3 Something Is Wrong with Dark Energy, Physicists Say by Rebecca Boyle (August 19, 2024); 3.1 Schizophrenia's Unyielding Mysteries by Michael Balter (May 1, 2017); 3.2 What's So Funny? The Science of Why We Laugh by Giovanni Sabato (June 26, 2019); 3.3 How Old Can Humans Get? by Bill Gifford (July 31, 2023); 4.1 What's the World's Oldest Language? by Lucy Tu (August 24, 2023); 4.2 War Is *Not* Part of Human Nature by R. Brian Ferguson (September 1, 2018); 4.3 Is Inequality Inevitable? by Bruce M. Boghosian (November 1, 2019); 4.4 The Theory That Men Evolved to Hunt and Women Evolved to Gather Is Wrong by Cara Ocobock & Sarah Lacy (November 1, 2023); 5.1 Volcanic Activity, Not Giant Bears, Created Enigmatic Devils Tower by Scott K. Johnson (March 10, 2015); 5.2 Ocean Discoveries Are Revising Long-Held Truths about Life by Timothy Shank (August 1, 2022); 5.3 'Dark Oxygen' Discovered Coming from Mineral Deposits on Deep Seafloor by Allison Parshall (July 22, 2024); 5.4 One Mystery of Stonehenge's Origins Has Finally Been Solved by Scott Hershberger (July 29, 2020); 5.5 King Tut Mysteries Endure 100 Years after Discovery by Zach Zorich (November 4, 2022).

Each author biography was accurate at the time the article was originally published.

Content originally published on or after July 1, 2018, was reproduced with permission. Copyright 2025 Scientific American, a Division of Springer Nature America, Inc. All rights reserved.

Content originally published from January 1, 2010, to June 30, 2018, was reproduced with permission. Copyright 2025 Scientific American, a Division of Nature America, Inc. All rights reserved.

Content originally published on or before December 31, 2009, was reproduced with permission. Copyright 2025 Scientific American, Inc. All rights reserved.

INDEX

A
agriculture, 14, 103, 106–107, 130
aliens, 5, 30–33, 35, 37, 41–43
Altman, Sidney, 8
Alzheimer's disease, 138
antimatter, 44–46, 50–60
apes, 24, 85, 111, 128
artificial intelligence (AI), 18
assembly theory, 39–40
astronomy, 5, 30, 49
attention-deficit hyperactivity disorder (ADHD), 16

B
behavior, 12, 16–17, 19, 25, 27, 92, 113, 128–129
    adaptive, 110
    disorders, 16
    patterns, 28–29
big bang, 40, 50, 61, 63, 65–66
biologists, 8, 19, 86, 91, 110, 138
biology, 5, 10, 31–39, 41, 73, 91, 95–96, 131, 143
bowhead whale, 92–94
brain
    and being funny, 89
    and empathy, 23, 26
    anomalies, 79
    big-brain vision of evolution, 12
    damage, 78
    development, 72–73
    disease, 76
    of a fetus, 80
    stem, 86

C
cancer, 73, 93–94, 96, 138
Carter, Howard, 147–148
Cech, Thomas, 8
chemosynthesis, 136
children, 15–18, 23–24, 78, 80, 122–123, 127
chimpanzees, 14, 102–103, 110–111
Church, Russell, 22–23, 85
Clarion-Clipperton Zone (CCZ), 139
cosmic inflation, 65
Cowan, Clyde Jr., 45

D
dark energy, 44, 61–67
death, 70, 93, 96, 104–106, 149, 152,
Devils Tower, 133
diseases, 12

DNA, 7-12, 30, 32-33, 38, 72, 81, 94-95, 129, 138, 151
dogs, 22, 24, 123,

E

Earth
   atmosphere, 8-9, 30
   early history, 7
   oceans, 8, 37, 132, 136-139, 142-143
economy, 114-117, 120, 152
Einstein, Albert, 55, 62-63
electrons, 37, 50-57, 59-60
epigenetics, 79
ethnography, 106, 108-109, 124,
Euclid space telescope, 66
Europa, 37-37

F

Freud, Sigmund, 84

G

genes, 8, 71-73, 75-79, 82, 89, 92-94, 138
   gene therapy, 17
   germ-line therapy, 17
   heritability, 16, 76, 80-82
geologists, 133, 144
geroscience, 92

H

Harpending, Henry C., 13-14
Hawks, John, 14

homicide, 102, 104
Hud, Nicholas, 10
human life span, 92, 95
human species, 12, 16, 18, 21
humor, 20, 48-49, 83-90

I

immune system, 72, 95

J

Japan, 75, 106, 123
Johnson, Sarah Stewart, 30-31, 35-38, 42-43
Jones, Steve, 15

K

Kidd Creek Mine, 37

L

Laboratory for Agnostic Biosignatures (LAB), 31-32
languages
   Afroasiatic, 99-100
   Chinese, 100
   dying, 98
   earliest documented writing, 99
   Sanskrit, 100
   Tamil, 100
laughter, 83-89
life
   definition, 32
   extraterrestrial, 30, 41
Los Alamos, 47-49

Index

M
Man the Hunter, 122–124, 130,
Mars, 31, 35–36, 138
Meadows, Victoria, 41–42
Miller, Stanley, 8
Mogil, Jeffrey S., 25
Murchison meteorite, 41

N
Nancy Grace Roman Space Telescope, 66
Neandertals, 128–129, 131
Nefertiti, 147, 149–151
neutrinos, 45–48, 66

O
Occam's razor, 27–28
oligarchy, 113, 116–118, 120

P
paleontologists, 13
parents, 15, 18, 78, 99
particle collider, 52, 54
Pauli, Wolfgang, 46–47
physics, 5, 34, 45, 49–51, 54, 60, 64, 113, 143
poverty, 77, 113, 117, 120
pregnancy, 80, 122–123, 131
Psychiatric Genomics Consortium (PGC), 71
psychologists, 22–23, 26, 75–76, 83, 88, 91

R
resolution of incongruity, 84
Riess, Adam G., 62–63, 65, 67
Riordon, James, 45
RNA, 7–9, 30, 32–34

S
schizophrenia, 70–75, 77–81
speed of light, 48, 55, 58
Standard Model, 50–54
Stonehenge, 132, 144–146
Sutherland, John, 7, 10–11, 34, 40
Switzer, Kathrine, 123

T
Thayer, Bradley, 103
Tourette's syndrome, 16
Tutankhamun (King Tut), 147–152
twins, 77, 81

U
universe, 5, 30, 33, 43, 45–46, 50–51, 60–67
Urey, Harold, 8

V
van Leeuwenhoek, Antonie, 35

W
wealth inequality, 114, 120

Z

Závada, Prokop, 133–137